The

Big Apple

Took A

Bite Off Me

Kim Lee

For my beautiful son, Noah.
May you live big, with meaning and purpose.
May your life's chapters be inked with rich and beautiful
experiences. I love you to the moon and back.

My darling friends Tim, Simon and Aya.
You were the colors to my technicolored life in NYC.
My sister and Angie, you are both my rock.
I love you all dearly.

P.S.: My son Noah is not part of the memoir, he was born years
later.

1

Preface

One day, I finally understood why the timing was perfect and why things had to happen exactly the way they did. I was guided to where I was always meant to be. The road that I had chosen and the experiences I had gone through led to my growth and evolution. This was all divine timing.

I procrastinated for 20 years to write this memoir, due to a myriad of reasonable reasons. At the time, I was prioritizing my young son and my work. I am a single mom, raising my son on my own for the past 13 years. I am the sole breadwinner for our tiny family of two.

I soared to great career heights, only to experience a dip afterwards. However, I fought my way back to the top again, only to later fall from grace. Life is full of ups and downs. My focus was always pulled into a vortex of my son's welfare, his needs, my work, the politics of my job, and the frequent work travels. Who has time to write a book? It required a serious commitment.

Once upon a time, to publish a book, you needed to have a rolodex of publisher and literary agent contacts, which I had none. I studied writing at City University of New York, which gave me an insight into the gauntlet of challenges that comes with writing. Fast forward decades and hallelujah, self-publishing became an option.

I look forward. I don't look back. The desire to write new chapters of my life held me back. I didn't want to write what was already written.

Last year, I made the difficult decision to resign from my workplace as a Chief Officer of two portfolios. Many of my team members also felt compelled to leave due to the unethical management practices that compromised our integrity, principles, and ethics.

It was a challenging time for me as my son was also going through a tough period, experiencing difficulties at school and causing disruptions that led to daily calls from his school principal and teachers. Given the mental strain I was under, I ultimately made the decision to take some time off.

The time has come for me to start a role. Not just any role, but a senior executive role. You can work out the odds of that. However, as I am well-weathered by the unpredictability of life, I have decided not to stress. It will come. Ask and you shall receive. Don't settle. Keep your eye on the prize. You are worth your weight in gold. These are the narratives and self-talk that run through my mind to sharpen my iron-clad will of waiting for that prized role.

So here I am, writing. It's like a gentle nudge from the universe, urging me to put my fingers to the keyboard. This blank space in front of me is just begging to be filled with words.

Twenty years back, I was having a laugh with my New York buddies, telling them I'd pen a book about my rather extraordinary experiences titled "The Big Apple Took a Bite off Me". My memoir would be a candid account of how I thought I'd take a big juicy bite off the Big Apple. But instead, I felt like the Big Apple took a big juicy bite off me.

My losses were staggering. It felt as though my naivete, career, hope, and faith, along with many other things dear to me, were taken away. I faced so many job rejections that I began to take them in stride, not even blinking an eye at the next one. After I left New York, I found myself facing a hefty credit card bill of $30,000, a result of hedonistic times I had indulged in. Over the next few years, I had to work on paying off this debt.

But she also gave me so much more back then. With

each pain, I grew stronger. My perspective on the world widened significantly. I saw and experienced outrageous things that I wouldn't have had the chance to if I had stayed within the comfort and confines of my home country. I became more experienced in life and more liberal in my views. My intuition was greatly sharpened. I made lifelong friends and had numerous fantastic memories and fun.

My buddies were in stitches over the title and thought that penning down the memoir was a stroke of genius. Years later, having bid adieu to the Big Apple, I found myself spinning yarns to captivated audiences back home and later in Amsterdam, my new home. I flirted with the idea of writing a book again, but I mastered the art of procrastination.

Fast forward two decades, here I am, attempting to paint a vivid picture from the palette of my memories. Striving for authenticity, rather than embellishment, was my aim. None of the characters and events are fictitious. I even decided to use the real names of my dear friends - Tim, Simon, and Aya. I wanted to bring back that warm, comforting blanket of familiarity.

I've altered the names of the other characters to respect their privacy and safeguard their identities. It's not my intention to upset or offend anyone, even though this is a kiss and tell kind of book. For me, the past is just that - the past. I harbor no regrets for my actions, as I view them as crucial in my personal growth and formation of my identity.

The purpose of my memoir was to recreate the vivid, technicolored experiences of my life in the Big Apple. I had moments of sweet delight, mixed in with some that were unpleasant. This was my lust-for-life and survivor story when I first set foot in New York, back in early 2001.

Post 9/11, I battled the odds to stay on in the intimidating Big Apple. It was not long until I discovered my LG - that's Lesbian Gay – tribe (I'm straight) and became a diamond runner in the Diamond District to make ends meet. Despite the increasingly stringent visa conditions, I managed to secure jobs in advertising, though I was eventually laid off due to prejudice.

On this journey, I encountered racism, gender bias, bullying, and a growing trend of xenophobia. All of these experiences were before the rise of the Woke Culture.

When *Sex and the City*, *Will & Grace*, and *Mad Men* were riding high on the wave of TV popularity, it felt like my life was running in parallel, with striking similarities. The only difference was that my life was unscripted.

This is my homage to all the marginalized and unsung

heroes who went to the Big Apple as starry-eyed kids with big dreams but fell through the cracks. Their stories deserved to be heard. To me, it's not the success but the courage to stay on and survive the Big Apple that matters. There is glory in failing. This is a book about how I found love, comfort in crisis, my place in a new world, and how I became stronger through setbacks and failures.

Everyone in my life in New York had to turn up, and every experience had to transpire for the creation of this book. I am grateful to my loved ones and even those who caused me pain. Each one had a lesson to teach me. Looking back on the turbulent times I've weathered, I'm comforted by the reminder that things will always be fine.

I truly enjoyed writing this book. Thoughts flew faster than the speed of typing. I found myself both basking in nostalgia and flinching at some of the old memories that resurfaced.

Thank you for being my audience. For you and my son are the reasons why I wrote this book. I wanted to share the intricate details of my life in New York with my son who has always shown a keen interest and fascination towards my childhood and the various phases of my life that I spent in Singapore, London, New York, and Amsterdam.

I sincerely hope that this book brings you something valuable, or at the very least, serves as a source of entertainment for you.

P.S.: Check out pictures and other titbits at

Instagram: #Bigappletookabiteoffme

Facebook: Big Apple Took a Bite Off Me

2

New York, New York

I packed my bags and hightailed them to the Big Apple in spring, a few months prior to September 11, 2001.

"Welcome to our new life in New York!" chirped Jai, his British accent crunching like a fresh apple in the Big Apple itself, as he chucked our Chelsea apartment door wide open. Jai was my North Indian, London-bred fiancé. "Honey, we are in New York!" He was clearly on a New York high.

Droopy-eyed and jet-lagged, I spent what felt like a lifetime - okay, 18 hours, but who's counting - flying from my sunny island of Singapore all the way to Newark Liberty International Airport. Jai picked me up at the airport and our cab ride through the city traffic felt longer than my flight.

Jai got a jump-start on me, landing in NYC a month earlier to kick off his new role as the Managing Director of a conference company in New York. He had just been upgraded from General Manager at their Singapore branch. This was an incredible opportunity for him. Ahem, for us. I was a little sore about this but put a pin in that – we'll circle back to this.

"Wow," I deadpanned, giving Jai a weak thumbs up. I was as tired as a snail on a treadmill, but I had to admit, our small apartment had charm. It was fully furnished with sleek furniture and carpeted too. I ran my fingers across the furniture to take in the newness of our new chapter. I then started rummaging through drawers and cabinets, oohing and aahing at the state-of-the-art kitchen equipment.

Glorious sunlight poured through the large windows that overlook the busy streets and filled the apartment with sunny optimism. Across us was a half-constructed building, destined to be a shiny skyscraper someday.

"That's the Empire State building. It shines brighter than a firefly at night," Jai gushed, pointing at the iconic structure from our window, evidently bitten by the excitement bug. He pranced me through the living room to the bedroom like a tour guide on a sugar rush. "Here's our bedroom. Check out the bed!" Jai pounced onto the bed with the energy of a five-year-old on a trampoline. "Well, what do you think?"

"I love it." The new place was sleek, shiny, and oh-so stylish. It was like stepping into one of those fancy home decor magazines. I could already imagine our old, cluttered apartment in Singapore shaking its head in disbelief. I could feel it in my hair follicles, this was the start of something so big and memorable.

"Don't get too attached. We're here only for three months," Jai gently warned. My imaginary balloon was burst with a prick of a pin. I was already planning on how to fully utilize the storage spaces. "Remember we are moving to SoHo?" he reminded me of our conversations on how we planned to live it up in New York. If not SoHo, where else?

Nightfall came fast. Maybe it was the jetlag, or the shorter day light hours. It was springtime, but the air bit like a teething puppy. After unpacking my bags, I swaddled myself in my brand new, brown, faux fur-trimmed coat and plopped a dapper blue flat cap atop my head. We galloped to the rooftop like caffeine-fueled crazies, ready to take in the twinkling expanse of the night city view.

There it was - The Empire State building lit up beautifully in white. As we stood there, looking like two marshmallows bundled up in our winter coats, we couldn't help but marvel at the overwhelming beauty of the awe-inspiring architecture.

Jai was 30. I was 25. This was all terribly spine-tingling for young guns like us. We only dreamed of living in New York

City. Later, we took a vacation and narrowly missed the 9/11 tragedy. We returned to rebuild our dream, right alongside our fellow New Yorkers.

I breathed in the cold chilly air that filled my lungs with warm hope. I wondered if people – tourists, transplants, immigrants and natives across the city, took in the view of the Empire State Building with the same silent wonderment. I drew in a deep breath and whispered in amazement, "New York, New York."

3

Stranger Things. Stranger Talk.

Soon, I found myself in a sea of boredom. I had no friends, partly by my own volition. My social circle consisted of a bunch of Singaporeans in the Big Apple, connections courtesy of my Singapore friends. But they were dull as dishwasher. So, in a plot twist surprising to no one, I ended up preferring my own company. I was hungry for fun and intellectual talk and boy, did I miss my buddies back home.

To add salt to the wound, I became a dependent. A semi-dependent, to be accurate. I'm the product of a low-income, dysfunctional family that somehow went from a trilogy to a saga when my half-brother popped onto the scene. My dad left when I was seven, leaving my mom to play both parenting roles without a single shiny penny from him.

It didn't take a genius to realize that my ticket out of the poverty express was to get a job that actually paid. My sister Kaylee, aka my economic guardian angel, helped keep my pockets filled during school, and I got a bank loan for my university fees.

After tossing my graduation cap, I single-handedly tackled my loan, using the dough I made from a hodgepodge of jobs. I've been everything from a private tutor to a sales assistant. Then, I landed a gig as a Sub-Editor for not one, but two mind-numbingly dull semi-conductor and automation magazines. Being a semi-dependent or dependent doesn't suit me well.

To stay in New York, I was granted a courtesy L-1A US Intra Company Transferee Visa with my former conference company, a sibling firm of Jai's. The icing on the cake? A cool grand, a courtesy fee for being a part-time consultant to the New York office. Catch is, I didn't even have to show up. This was all part of our relocation deal. You might be thinking this is a pretty solid arrangement, and you'd be right. The monthly allowance funded my New York City daily adventures.

Jai and I were thrown together by destiny in a shared office space in Singapore. We were like two peas in a pod, except we worked at sister companies. I was a Conference Producer and resigned the day our London-based Global Managing Director decided to grace us with her presence. We had an inept Managing Director from London, Kelly, in charge of the Singapore office.

Our star of the show, always fashionably late to work with a hangover that could rival a rockstar's. Often politically incorrect, she couldn't mask her disdain for Asians. She sprinkled condescension on us, seemingly forgetting the era of colonialism was a thing of the past. Nearing her fifties, single and without kids, bitterness ate at her like vultures feeding off a corpse.

At these conference events, her inner glutton always seemed to take the wheel. There she'd be, first in line, making a mountain out of mashed potatoes and chicken wings on her plate like she was preparing for hibernation. She'd munch away, chomping, even when she was talking. It was like watching a nature documentary on pigs - in business attire. One day, I finally reached the end of my rope with her absence of dignity and decorum.

I got all prepped up to say adios to my job. After wrapping up all my work, I arranged them neatly into one file and presented it to Sally, our globe-trotting super boss, during our private one-on-one meet. She seemed impressed by my strategic thinking and meticulous work. Then, with a dramatic flourish, I handed over my resignation letter.

As cool as a cucumber, as she always was, she asked for the reasons. I spilled the beans, all over the table. "Give me 24 hours," she almost whispered, and flipped the resignation letter back at me. I was as clueless as a goldfish about what was about to go down next.

The next day, she swooped down to my humble desk and asked for a few minutes in the meeting room. "Look, I called up our global CEO last night, and we have decided to promote you to Director. We will first send you to London for management training. Thereafter, you can pick any of our offices worldwide to work at. Let me know what you think by tomorrow. We'll iron out all the details." Kelly? She was demoted and sent back to London. Bye, greedy birdy.

There I was, my brain all mushy, rooted to my chair like a tree. I was about to scram and start fretting over my next measly paycheck, and I get promoted? And they're sending me where? Just a year out of the university, some of my friends were working at call centers, while others were on a wild goose chase for jobs that seemed to be playing a never-ending game of hide and seek. But then, out of the blue, here comes this news, all dolled up like a Christmas present. Felt like the universe just handed me a giant, shiny gift.

I was so full of good news, I unloaded them on Jai. Instead of joining my happy dance, he just sat there like a grumpy cat. Undeterred, and still practically levitating with joy, I snuck into a meeting room and dialed up my buddies to blabber about the news I received that morning. Predictably, they were jumping over the moon with joy for me.

I usually burnt the midnight oil at work. But on this particular evening, I darted out of the office at the stroke of quitting time. With a hop, skip, and a jump, I made a beeline to the bar across the street, where my friends were already gathered, ready to raise a toast. We called it a night early, as I needed to respond to Sally's oh-so-generous offer. New York was going to be my choicest pick of office to work at, and it wasn't a hard decision to make.

At the ripe hour of 4 AM, Jai came wobbling home, stinking like a distillery. He'd been out with his two best buddies. If the saying "A drunk mind speaks a sober heart" is true, then Jai's heart was belting out a heartfelt song. He didn't want me to take up that job offer, as he couldn't leave the Singapore office. Suddenly, it felt like his career had VIP access and mine was stuck backstage. I was left juggling between leaving or staying.

The next morning, I caught Sally right before she zoomed off to London. I thanked her for the out-of-this-world offer. I explained that I would gladly accept the promotion and management training in London but would be returning to the Singapore office thereafter. So, there I was, with my career simmering on the back burner, while I tossed my one-way ticket to the Big Apple into a black hole of regret.

A month later, I zipped off to London. I was shacked up in a swanky serviced apartment in South Kensington, and had a blast exploring the museums, diving headfirst into the nightlife, feasting my eyes on the sights, and soaking up the culture. After a few glorious months, I found myself reluctantly shuffling my feet back to Singapore. I was gnawed at by lament, feeling stuck.

One fine day, I finally resigned. I thanked Sally for the life-changing opportunities, then moonwalked into advertising as a Creative Copywriter at one of the most prestigious agencies in the world.

A year had passed, and Jai got a promotion and an offer from the Big Apple. And there I was, still nursing my bruised ambitions, which I had willingly put on the back burner for him. The plan was for me to be there, on my own terms, living the life I'd always fantasized about. But no, I was stuck living his dream instead. "We are now living our dream," he'd say, trying to correct me.

I'm not about to roast Jai like a Thanksgiving turkey, he was one heck of a guy. His resume was a buffet of impressive traits: well-educated, great manners, smart as a whip, loving and generous. I had the freewill to choose, and I picked him over New York.

Most days in New York, the only person I get to gab with was Jai, after he was done with work. I was intrigued yet intimidated by the sassy and confident way New Yorkers spoke. Back in my hometown, we don't do small talk. You try to chat up a local, and they'd either stare at their shoes, check out the sky, or straight up pretend you're invisible. So don't be fooled by our shiny tourist brochures, we aren't the friendliest nation.

Mind you, I'm no shrinking violet. Plucky, playful, cheeky and vocal, a hearty chat was my cup of tea. A globetrotter and backpacker, I've rubbed shoulders with folks from all walks of life. But when it came to small talk or mingling with strangers in the Big Apple, those folks were simply in a class by themselves.

One fine day, smack in the middle of a sun-soaked afternoon, Jai and I were chilling out at Central Park. Following the age-old New York tradition, Jai abandoned me temporarily to raid a hotdog stand. While I was on my lonesome, a Black man ambled over to me. He had a bone to pick with George W. Bush's latest blooper.

I was stuck in my tracks like a deer in headlights. He rattled off at the speed of a runaway train. I stood there, the epitome of patience and politeness, listening to his impassioned rant. Every now and then, I'd bob my head and slip in a "uh-huh" whenever he paused to take a breath.

Jai galloped towards me, two hotdogs perched precariously on flimsy napkins that fluttered in the breeze. He cut in like a needle going off a spinning record. I blinked at him, my face a painting of confusion, while my brain frantically tried to decode his rudeness. He yanked me away from the chattering gentleman I was talking to.

"Hun. He's homeless." Jai said, casually biting into his sausage like it was the juiciest gossip. "Huh?" I blinked, my brows knitting together. We haven't got homeless people in Singapore, so I didn't know what he was talking about.

"He was going on about George W. Bush. He knew what he was talking about." I defended the man. I shot a cheeky glance to the man, doing a double take for dramatic effect. At that moment, with all the flair of a magician pulling a rabbit out of a hat, he plucked a crinkled edition of The New York Times from a handy bin. He gave the headline a good once-over before diving deep into the articles.

I eyeballed him up and down, taking in the dirt-encrusted clothes and those worn-out feet that had clearly seen more miles than a second-hand taxi cab. His hair was a salt and pepper knot-fest that would give a flared-up Medusa a run for her money. Welcome to New York, where the reality hits you hard in your gut.

It took a while before I could chat up strangers without breaking a sweat. This one time, I was just moseying down the street when this beefy, bald, Black guy, decided to strike up a convo with me. He started jabbering away in this thick New York accent that was so charming.

Man: "Hey China doll!"

Me: "Hey back!"

Man: "Where you from, China doll?"

Me: "Singapore."

Man: "A'ight. Shanghai? Ah been to Shanghai too!"

It was a short exchange but at least I found my confidence and my voice.

4

Eye Candy by the Windows

Remember the big windows that let generous sunlight into our Chelsea apartment? They also offered a generous view of my new breathtaking world.

Our apartment was perched on the eighth floor, a perfect vantage point to peep out of our windows into the concrete jungle beneath. The streets were a never-ending parade of chaos, trapped in a loop of time. This resulted in a low-grade, 24/7 hullabaloo that seeped in, even when the windows were firmly shut.

Picture this: an orchestra of never-ending car honks, serenades from police cars and fire trucks, and a sprinkling of colorful language that would make a sailor blush. Add to that, the symphony of spontaneous laughter, inebriated singing belted out at top decibels, especially post the witching hour. And don't forget the piercing whistles of cabbies being hailed, children's screams, and a variety of other noises. These were the sounds that made up our daily soundtrack.

I used to get a real kick out of parking myself in front of the windows to soak up all the non-stop action. Move aside NY1 news. This was New York live TV. It was an all-you-can-eat visual buffet. And then, like a cherry on top of my sundae, I discovered new eye candy by the windows.

Each weekday morning, I waited with bated breath for Jai to take off for work. I'd pull an Oscar-worthy performance of being lost in dreamland while he got ready. The very second I heard the sweet melody of the door locking after his disappearing silhouette, I'd kicked the tangled sheets off and spring out of bed with a messianic determination.

I hopped into the shower, barely letting the water warm up before I was under it. Then, like an Olympic sprinter, I glanced at the clock. In a fit of fashion madness, I wrestled with a handful of dresses before one finally tapped out and was deemed the winner. I took a moment to admire my reflection in the mirror. I playfully tossed my hair to the side, cranking up the sass factor to 11. I filled a mug with enough coffee to make a barista sweat. With a casual swagger, I strolled into the living room, coffee mug in hand. Then, with all the grace, I collapsed onto the comfy sofa, my eyes drinking in the view from the massive windows. And like clockwork, I performed this chaotic ballet every weekday by 9 in the morning. Well, by then, they'd all have started work.

By 'they', I'm referring to the legion of sizzling, beefcake builders flexing their muscles at the skyscraper construction site just across the street. Our windows framed them like a live action movie, in high-definition view. Covertly drooling over these dashing, rugged men perched on the scaffolding, swinging their biceps, became my new hobby.

Come summer, I crumbled like sand at the windows. There were those who went shirtless, parading around in skin-tight tees or tank tops, so moist with sweat. Then there were the guys in jeans so tight, I lost my breath every time they bent over. And let's not forget the ones who rocked those frayed shorts, showcasing thighs that could be mistaken for tree trunks. Cue in Bananarama's *Cruel Summer* song.

The epitome of masculinity in motion, these guys were tanned, taut, and oozing sex appeal. It was like watching a live performance of an erotic poem. Lust wasn't just inevitable, it was unavoidable. My windows turned into a real-life version of Playgirl magazine. Instead of static images, I had a front row seat to a display of strutting, working, glistening male bodies.

I was languorously tormented by a burning desire. We were stuck on opposite sides of a window, but that glass was of no barrier. Some days, they'd send waves my way, other days, they'd wolf-whistle. And on the really good days? They'd blow kisses that made me feel like I'd just won the lottery. I'd play it cool, smiling back, but inside, I was more like a popcorn kernel in a microwave.

Did I emotionally cheat? I stumbled upon this term one fine day when I was reading an article about it. Apparently, emotional cheating is a form of cheating. So, if that's the case, I was bloody guilty as charged. I was like a kid with my nose pressed against the candy store window. Those hunky men outside were my sweet guilty pleasure.

It was unfair to compare Jai with the sex gods out there. He started losing hair when he was only in his twenties. By the time he blew out the candles on his 30th birthday cake, his head was as shiny as a bowling ball. Dark skinned and tubby with a beer belly, he looked more Brazilian than North Indian. He wasn't a sex symbol, but he had an infectious smile.

For two whole months, I was on a visual diet of these sizzling, smoking, hot-to-trot hunks which woke up my snoozing libido. Meanwhile, Jai ceased to be attractive to me.

5

From Chelsea to SoHo

SoHo, you ask? Oh, darling, it stands for South of Houston, just a fun fact you might've missed among all the city's hustle and bustle.

After a three-month, drool-filled, eye-candy binge for me in Chelsea, we took our fabulous selves downtown. Yes, to a loft so spacious it could fit my shoe collection - nestled right in the heart of Varick, sandwiched between Grand and Watts Street, in the southernmost tip of SoHo. And just like that, I transformed into a downtown girl.

Tell most people you live in SoHo and watch their eyes expand like they've just downed a shot of adrenaline. There is always this dramatic pause, followed by an almost reverential whisper, "That's so cool." Super cool it was for me and forever will be. I have a beautiful chapter of my life inked in SoHo that cannot be erased. It's like a standout chapter in my life's novel, still going strong after two decades.

Defining SoHo is a tricky as defining New York City.

For some, it's all glitz and glamour, a place where even the sidewalks seem to be strutting down a catwalk. For others, it's all about the bling-bling. Then there are those who see SoHo as a hub of creativity, where every street corner is a potential art installation, and every café conversation is a brainstorming session for the next big thing. It's a bit offbeat, a bit left field, and full of surprises. And let's not forget its celebrity obsession. If you tripped over a rock in SoHo, it's probably because you were too busy gawking at a movie star.

SoHo is the ultimate shopping mecca for fashion pilgrims around the globe. It's a magnet for those who swear by obscure indie labels, can't resist the allure of glitzy chain stores, or have a serious obsession with the crème de la crème of the fashion world - think Gucci, Prada, Christian Dior, and Chanel. These pilgrims form their own holy grail of queues outside these fashion temples from the crack of dawn till the stars pop out.

Mind you, not everyone gets in. You've got to spiff up and look moneyed. Once, I was with an ex-colleague turned friend, Stan, standing in one of those never-ending lines outside Gucci. We waited for two hours that felt like an eternity, only to have the suited-up, no-nonsense bouncer, give Stan's checkered shirt and chino pants the once over.

Stan was deemed wielding reduced buying power and got the old heave-ho. In solidarity, I gave up on my entry too. For Stan, it became a lifelong shopping bane he was never to recover from. He was permanently scarred.

My trusted fashion hotspots were more down to earth and less stressful - Anthropologie, Banana Republic, H&M, Nike, Gap, Victoria's Secret and many more that I can barely recall. I would lose whole days lost in the warren of narrow streets, popping into store after store like a kid on a candy spree. Broadway was akin to the Great Wall of China of shopping streets. You can easily spend an entire day shopping there.

I stumbled upon these jazzy stores in SoHo that I'd never even heard of before. They quickly became as essential as my morning coffee during my SoHo saunters. Crate and Barrel wasn't just a furniture store to me. It was and still is a destination that you head to when you have arrived in life and desire a luxe upgrade of your home with gorgeous furniture, fabulous home and kitchen bling.

Dean and DeLuca, which has since shuttered in SoHo, wasn't just a supermarket to me. It was a glorious symphony of food and delicacies. I remember it like it was yesterday, stepping into that grocery wonderland for the first time. It was like walking straight into a buffet for the senses. I threw my glance up to the ceiling that was cathedral high. Chatters of the elbow-to-elbow jostling crowd rose to great heights and filled the store.

To the left of the cavernous store, there was a never-ending lineup of counters serving up freshly prepared takeaway food. The dishes were so temptingly delicious, they practically threw themselves into your cart begging to be taken home. The hard part was deciding which ones to buy.

A bit further down the line stood a bakery display that was so presidential – Pastries, cookies, and cakes were crafted with such finesse, it's like the bakers were trying to one-up God when he whipped up Adam and Eve. This was my favorite section, hands down. It was a smorgasbord of sugar and glory, boasting a dizzying selection of the most over-the-top cakes you can imagine. We're talking birthday cakes, wedding cakes, anniversary cakes, "I-just-got-axed-from-my-job" cakes, "my-cat-kicked-the-bucket-but-I've-got-a-rebound-feline" cakes, and any other life event your cake-crazy brain hasn't even fathomed yet. They literally had it all.

Then they had these sky-high metal shelves just brimming with foodstuffs that were so swanky, I hadn't even heard of them in my fresh-faced youth. There were 30 varieties of sea salt – who knew the sea had so much to offer? Then there were 76 kinds of peppers, because apparently 'spicy' isn't a one-size-fits-all. And don't get me started on those highfalutin seasonings. Plus, they had honey from bees that had been dining on nothing but organic nibbles. I was so gob smacked by the kaleidoscope of posh, top-drawer, and discerning products.

My shopping addiction was so intense, that our loft soon looked like a hidden treasure trove of unused, glittering goodies. I had more winter coats than a Siberian or Russian. And let's not forget the shoes. I was strutting around with a hundred pairs of shoes, despite having only two humble feet to wear them with.

SoHo was the hotspot for all the swanky art galleries. The openings were a riot - a real circus of artsy, eccentric and outlandishly clad individuals who would be spilling out onto the cobblestones, their faces turning as red as the overpriced wine they were guzzling. It was like people-watching on steroids. Far from minted, I could never afford art sold at the art galleries, but I quickly buddied up with some artists and before I knew it, I had invitations to art parties and openings.

SoHo hosts some of the world's best eateries, waterholes, and coffee nooks. I'd love to list them all here, but I have other stories to write. Reading a SoHo restaurant review in the New York Times for me is like reading Fifty Shades of Gravy. By the end of it, you're drooling and fully turned on for more.

SoHo seemed to shrink with each passing day, what with all the locals, tourists, celebs, and die-hard New York aficionados flooding the streets. I was constantly stopped in my tracks by people asking for directions. This one time, and I know it's a bit naughty, I sent a gaggle of blondes from the Midwest on a wild goose chase. They had the audacity to interrupt my super important phone call at a traffic light.

It wasn't always pretty in SoHo. When the moon clocked in for its night shift, the homeless community got cozy with their couture cardboard beds sprawled across the cobblestone catwalk. Often, they'd pool their pennies from generous pedestrians to score some bargain booze, and drank till they passed out. Some nights, they'd take up phantom boxing or chatter away to an invisible audience. At times, pointless fights broke out amongst them. And sometimes, they just sat, lost in a world of their own. Over time, I'd grown used to them. Among these urban survivalists, one character was especially unforgettable.

On a scorcher of a summer day, there I was,

sauntering out of my local deli, gnawing on a New York delicacy that had stolen my heart - a smoked salmon and cream cheese bagel. Suddenly, up wobbled a disheveled homeless. Instinctively, my hand dove into my pocket for some jingly-jangly spare change, all the while my other hand was devoted to protecting the last precious bite of my beloved salmon cream cheese bagel.

I triumphantly presented a handful of coins, but to my surprise, he simply shook his head and, with a grubby finger that had seen better days, pointed at my prized bagel. "I want a smoked salmon and cream cheese bagel. I want what you're having." I was struck dumb. "Come on," he nagged. "OK. OK. Gimme a few minutes," I replied.

With a pinch of harassment in the air, I obediently did an about-face, and made tracks for the deli, still shaking my head over his peculiar demand. Just as I was about to sashay into the store, he let out another belly-shaking shout. "Oi, don't forget the caviar on the bagel!"

That homeless man was quite the character. He did score points on originality.

6

When Kim Met Tim

One of the most fabulous things that happened to me in New York was when I met Tim, who quickly became my Big Apple bestie. Much like a classic Big Apple pie, Tim was a bit crusty on the outside, but incredibly sweet on the inside. An outrageously gay unicorn, he brought even more color and vibrancy to my already technicolored life, proudly embodying all six colors of the LGBT pride flag.

Tim was always up for anything really and easily got excited about everything. Together, we had created a plethora of hilarious and silly memories that would last us several lifetimes.

Tim is one of my most loyal and steadfast friends. When it rains, it pours. He weathered all my storms with me in the Big Apple – he cushioned my every heart break, bought me meals when I was down to my last dime, offered a comforting shoulder during my darkest hours. His fabulous sense of humor never failed to crack me up. Not only did he help me bring out my best attributes, but he also helped me find and embrace my true self.

Recently, I had the pleasure of vacationing with Tim and his long-time partner, Simon, right in the heart of London. Even though they're still based in New York, the distance has never dulled our friendship. You know how they say there are friends and there is family, and then there are friends who become family? Well, that's exactly how I would describe Tim and Simon.

We were due for a reunion for quite some time, particularly after the COVID-19 pandemic threw everyone's travel plans into disarray. Sure, we've kept in touch through calls, but they simply can't compare to those treasured in-person moments filled with laughter and silliness.

The gathering was a perfect chance for Simon to meet my teenage son, Noah, for the first time. The last time Tim held Noah's hand, he was just a lively three-year-old toddler. Now, time has flown by and Noah is already 13 years old.

On June 1, 2023, we exchanged over-the-top kisses and hugs over a gorgeous dinner at OXO Tower Restaurant, Bar and Brasserie, housed in an award-winning landmark building in South Bank, with an iconic view of River Thames and St. Paul's. We swopped the spectacular New York skyline where we last dined, for the unparalleled views of the city of London. The backdrops may have changed, but the chemistry was still off the charts.

The stunning venue was picked by my good friend Pauline. She's been living it up in the UK for a few years now and she's got quite the knack for finding the ritziest spots. She pranced into the dinner, and surprised us with a bonus guest, our British friend, who used to live in Singapore but moved back to the land of tea and crumpets. Quite the gathering, really – a mixed bag of old friends and fresh faces.

Time does its time flying thing but Tim, Simon and I are exactly the way we were. We may be more wrinkled and packed on more pounds, but underneath those laugh lines and love handles are the same cheeky personalities.

A shared history is invaluable. A shared history of outrageous stories gathered through the thick-and-thin years is even more so. Tim and Simon started reminiscing our old Big Apple stories to a fresh audience. I had buried most of the stories deep in the forgotten vault. Everyone was in stitches after hearing the stories. Noah, the poor jet-lagged soul, even managed to pass out right on the table. But not before he had his fill of wild stories about his mom as bedtime stories.

When Noah and I returned from our holiday

extravaganza - a whirlwind tour of London, Bath, Edinburgh, Porto, and Lisbon, I felt everything had perfectly aligned in divine timing. So, I finally buckled down to business. Like our reunion that was long-due, this memoir was also long-due. It was time to dust off those stories and chapter them.

Tim and I bumped into each other at this wild LG bash in the heart of Chelsea. Now, back in those days, we were all about the rainbows and unicorns, totally submerging ourselves in the vibrant gay and lesbian scene. How we got that golden ticket to the party, I've got no clue, but Jai and I rocked up there anyway. Jai was a straight as an arrow and looked like a fish out of water at this party. I nudged him into the fabulous world of more colors than just black and white. You see, I grew up amidst lesbians, so the LGBTQ+ world and all its glorious diversity is familiar to me.

New to the party scene in Manhattan? There were these three questions that constantly popped up at every event. Manhattanites either open with these questions or somehow worm their way to them. Your responses steer the trajectory of the conversation. It either tragically dries up or magically flows on, blossoming into a friendship or relationship. Think of these as 'filter' questions asked at speed dating.

The trio of ultimate queries at a Manhattan party, in a jumbled order are:

1. What do you do?
2. How much do you pay for rent?
3. Where do you live?

The last question is employed mostly as an 'instant death' opening question. Let's be clear though, I wasn't the mastermind behind these rules, I might not have gotten them right. And the explanations? Well, let's just say they might have had a little touch of unfairness. So, before you go blaming me, remember who's just the messenger here.

For those not from the Big Apple, let me enlighten you. In Manhattan, your address isn't just your address, it's a full-blown biography. It's a bit hasty and unfair, but that's how it rolls there. Your hood is like your resume - it hints at your pocket size, your social standing, hobbies, traits, and even your quirks. It's like a cheat sheet for finding common ground with other folks. Searching for your perfect match? Well, your address can help you weed out the duds from the studs.

As a true-blue Manhattanite, I used to hang out only with my fellow borough-dwellers. Some of us would even restrict ourselves to our own neighborhoods for sheer convenience. Ever watch that hilarious sitcom *Seinfeld*? There's this one episode I remember, where Kramer finally steps out of his Upper West Side bubble and ventures downtown to Chinatown. He comes back with an "I Love New York" T-shirt, acting like he'd just returned from a full-on, out-of-town day trip.

When I lived in SoHo, I shopped till I dropped, dined like a queen, partied like a rockstar and got wasted like a college freshman. I laughed, cried, dreamed big and crashed even bigger - all in the heart of SoHo. Sure, I ventured out, only for work or for the occasional parties, bar or club hops.

We're about to take a jaunt through the jumble of Manhattan neighborhoods in the 2000s. Now remember, this is just for fun. Don't come at me with your pitchforks and torches if I poke a little fun at your neighborhood. I've based these stereotypes on my own wild escapades, along with some tall tales from my buddies.

The Upper East and Upper West Side, where the air is filled with a distinct aroma of superiority. Here, you'll find the nouveau riche and the old money folks, all born with silver spoons so shiny, you'd need sunglasses to look at them. There's a certain charm to their old and faded glamour, kind of like your grandma's floral wallpaper that's seen better days. You'll notice the over-the-top display of wealth, like flaunting a gold-plated toilet seat, or on the flip side, penny-pinching so intense, they'll reuse a tea bag more times than you can count.

The young males are a breed of their own, usually of the frat or preppy variety. Their wardrobes are predictable - tennis sweaters, Nantucket red pants, khakis, Polo Tees, blue blazers, and boat shoes. It's like they all shop at the same Upper East or Upper West side frat boutique.

Sure, they're well-educated but they can be as snooty as a cat looking down on a dog. They live by the old adage 'birds of a feather flock together', choosing to hang out or pair up exclusively with their own Upper East or Upper West side comrades. Sort of like a very exclusive, very expensive club.

SoHo and Tribeca, they are like the Kardashians of New York's neighborhoods. Always dressed in the latest fashion, probably even setting the trends. They are quirky enough to make a flamingo look dull.

Their moods swing more than a jazz band's rhythm section. One moment they're shallow and flashy, the next they're indulging in the finer things of life like a cat with a bowl of cream. They are the life of the party, always loud and gregarious, probably the ones starting the conga line.

And the best part? They are like a giant melting pot of

cultures, attracting everyone from the artistic hipsters to the gourmet foodies. In SoHo and Tribeca, every day is a fashion show.

Chelsea is the laidback cousin of SoHo who traded in their paintbrushes for rainbow flags. Don't get me wrong, Chelsea has its fair share of art and fashion. They're both cool in their own ways, but if you're all about that shop-till-you-drop lifestyle, SoHo might be your winner.

Let's dive into the eclectic, hipster-infused world of the Lower East Side and East Village. On the sunny side of the street, we've got the positives:

• Artsy fartsy folks

• Mellow yellow, chilled to the max, as laid back as a reclining chair.

• Deep thinkers, philosophers, and the occasional brooding poet.

• Wardrobe? Think Mark Zuckerberg on a laundry day.

On the flip side, we've got a few quirks:

• Inferiority complex. They're like the middle child of the city.

• Emotional rollercoasters. One minute they're Picasso, the next they're Eeyore.

- Penny pinchers. They can squeeze a nickel until the buffalo screams.

- Reliability? As stable as a three-legged chair.

- And let's not forget the struggling artists, turning ramen noodles into a gourmet meal. They couldn't afford the rent in a shoebox in the rest of the city.

At parties, I'd pull a Houdini on anyone from Staten Island, Queens, Brooklyn (except for Williamsburg) and New Jersey. A +212 (New York area code) incoming call display over a +732 (New Jersey area code) was preferred. It's shallow but we were all guilty of it.

I turned my nose up at Upper East Siders and Upper West Siders. First, I made small talk with them. Then tapered off and finally slithered off to load up on copious amounts of drinks. I immediately cozied up to anyone from SoHo, Tribeca and Chelsea. I was on the fence with those who lived in Midtown, Lower East Side, East Village and Williamsburg in Brooklyn.

Circling back to Tim. When we first met, sparks flew. Our conversation flowed as easy as free-flow champagne at a boozy brunch. Tim hails from a cozy small village just a stone's throw from Kuala Lumpur, in Malaysia. Like most gays, he was confused in his growing years and dated girls as a sort of 'hetero-dry run.' When he was a young adult, he decided to leave his religiously strict country where homosexuality is frowned upon and pursue his university education in Louisiana.

From there, he sashayed his way to the Big Apple, ready to let his rainbow flag fly high. The Big Apple took a few chomps out of Tim, but he is the living definition of resilience, laughing off every tumble and always bouncing back, ready for the next round.

An accountant at an insurance company, Tim lived in the Upper West Side. I bent my no Upper-West-Side rule for him which was well worth the rare exception because he is that funny and fabulous.

"Call me tomorrow, darling!" he drunk-slurred in his cute 'Magaysian' - hybrid of Malaysian and gay - accent. "Love you too!" I blew him exaggerated air kisses. The rest is history.

7

The Gang

Soon, we had a gang. When I first bumped into Tim at the party, he had two Malaysian friends in tow – Claire, who is lesbian and Sid, who is gay.

Let's start with Claire. She was a bore. Her presence and absence didn't make a difference. We were never sure what to make of her, but we were absolutely certain about two things - she took in air and took up space.

Claire and I have absolutely nothing in common. You'd have an easier time squeezing water from stones than getting a conversation going with her. Materialistic, dull, insipid, risk-adverse, mundane, ever-complaining, deeply insecure and supremely penny pinching. I'm going straight for the jugular, but these are some of the traits that best describe her. The last trait is my biggest pet peeve in life. It drove me up the wall when she constantly whined about how expensive things were. Hello girlfriend, it's New York City.

Tall, unattractive and plump, her long, black as tar

hair was the only whisper of femininity. She was always swimming in loose shirts and baggy pants. Her overall aura was odd and uncomfortable.

Sid was an improved version of Claire. Pint-sized and quiet, like Claire, with nothing much to offer when it came to interests and conversations. Sid was a waiter at several fancy restaurants including the famed Nobu. He made a killing on tips and once let slip that Robert De Niro was the best tipper at Nobu.

Once, I analyzed this trio's friendship from the sidelines. Their chatter flowed like Niagara Falls when they switched from English to Cantonese. As reserved and introverted as they usually were, Sid and Claire got talkative when they bitched, gossiped or grumbled.

I found myself inventing two categories for the adjective 'bitchy' - "Bitchy bitchy" and "Peachy bitchy". Now, "Bitchy bitchy" was the kind of term you'd use for someone who is vitriolic, malicious, backstabbing, manipulative and spiteful. On the other hand, "Peachy bitchy" was the fun cousin at the family reunion - the one who was bitchy in a fun, witty, lighthearted, and humorous way.

Claire and Sid are "bitchy bitchy" but not backstabbing nor spiteful. Tim is a "peachy bitchy". The two of them mostly jangled on Tim's nerves.

Thankfully we had perkier members like coupled-up Vinny and Thaddeus, hosts of fun gay parties such as the one where Tim and I met. Thaddeus, the 'top' in their relationship, is a second-generation Taiwanese Asian American born in the city. Vinny, on the other hand, is of Italian ancestry and from Upstate New York. They were stylish, witty, sassy and funny. Add to that a keen interest in politics and pop culture, and you've got the life of every party. Like bees to honey, I was drawn to them. And even after they decided to uncouple, Vinny stuck around.

Then there's Sud. Sud is from Singapore and of North Indian heritage. We got connected through a mutual friend in Singapore who thought, "These two need to meet."

A corporate lawyer and closeted gay at work, Sud was afraid of the political ramifications if he came clean with his sexuality. By day, he was a sharp-suited lawyer but when the office lights dim, he trades his power suit for fabulous flair and a glittering personality. Clean cut, stylish, smooth, composed, down to earth, cheeky with a wicked sense of humor, bright, articulate, westernized and knowledgeable. Those are some of his fabulous traits.

Don't be fooled by his intellectual front. Sud was a

secret connoisseur of all things pop trash. He had the latest lowdowns on Paris Hilton, Britney Spears, Jennifer Lopez, or any other celebrities who hugged the news headlines. Quick-witted, he often made snide and snarky remarks about Claire and Sid, right under their oblivious noses, much to my delight. Sud is "peachy bitchy".

There we were, the nucleus of the gang, with a few fringe friends who drifted in and out. Some even got the boot, like Kay. A total "bitchy bitchy" drama queen from Singapore, he had a penchant for name-dropping, backstabbing and constant tooting of his own horn. We'd roll our eyes so much around him, you'd think we were auditioning for a remake of *The Exorcist*. Tim absolutely abhorred him and eventually gave him the boot from the gang.

I couldn't resist but share a scandalous, tragic story about Kay's ex-boyfriend. Kay once dated this lovely man, Billy, who was already knocking on fifty's door when we were mostly in our roaring 20s. For all of Kay's shortcomings – and they were voluminous - Billy made up for them with charm, intelligence, grace, suave and refined manners.

According to Kay, Billy had more than a few skeletons in his closet. He was Jewish, pretend straight and married to a nice Jewish woman, like a good boy should. But here's the kicker - Billy is gay and was just trying to play by the old family, religion and societal rule book. A very successful realtor, he made a fortune for himself. When his three kids were grown up, he decided it was high time he stopped playing hide and seek with his sexuality. That was the start of his slippery slope.

His ex-wife was livid when she found out he'd been stringing her along. I mean, it's one thing when your man leaves you, but when he leaves you because he's gay, that's unforgivable. At least by her books. Kay told us that not only did she file for a divorce, but because she was so well-connected with the high society, she managed to wrest every bit of fortune Billy had. He was completely bankrupted – financially and mentally. It didn't end there.

To make ends meet and to keep up with the hefty alimony payments to his ex-wife, Billy decided to become a social escort. Billy wasn't anywhere near good looking. He had a face most fitting for a niche villainous role in a Western film. His skin, weathered and wrinkled like a well-used leather saddle, gave him a rodeo look. He looked like life had dealt him a bad card, but he had the right hide to deflect all misfortunes. And let's not forget about his physique - Billy was built like a brick house.

One time, he serviced a gay orgy in Amsterdam and ended up with a HIV positive status. On his uppers, he couldn't afford his medication. To get around that, he volunteered as a clinical trial and study participant in a university research. It didn't end there.

Billy went on to become a gay porn star. We didn't see him around anymore, apparently, he was too busy with his 'performances'. Anyway, we were having one of our usual parties at Vinny and Thaddeus's place when I just couldn't help but mention how much I missed Billy. Thaddeus, ever the joker, quickly quipped back, "Oh well. If you really want to see him, you can always head to Blockbuster and rent his porn movie!". As insensitive as it sounded, we couldn't help but burst into laughter.

I felt pangs of guilt after. Billy was a decent chap, trying to cobble whatever he could to put bread on the table. Moreover, he never griped about anything - his past, his ex, his escort or porn star work, or his struggles. He remained firmly upbeat even though his life took a very tragic and unconventional steer. Sadly, we stopped seeing him after Kay broke up with him. With Billy gone, we quickly bade adieu to Kay too.

Everyone in the gang was vastly different in character

and had different professions, but we were strung together by this crazy, star-spangled dream of ours. The Big Apple was our fertile ground of opportunities and freedom. For the rainbow brigade, it was where they could be fully accepted for their sexual orientation and find love.

There were times when the LG scene was too much for Jai and he shied away from most parties. But I would show up solo and have a whale of a time with the crew. Off we'd go to parties, like a flock of party-loving birds, we'd separate, mingle, belt out our three questions, and even recruit new blood to join our merry band. As the party reached its twilight, we'd gather back together like bees to a hive. We've ticked off the list of countless dinners, Sunday brunches, bar and club hops (both straight and gay because we're all about that diversity), home parties and of course, we'd never miss the chance to show our support at gay pride parades.

One of our favorite spots was Dallas BBQ, an American chain BBQ restaurant that still serves up gob-smacking American classics. Nowhere near spiffy or swanky, we were drawn to these cocktails served in massive goblets. You'll need two strong hands to lift these bad boys. In the mood to get drunk? Add an extra shot in a test-tube that's jammed into the goblet. No one in the gang could humanly polish more than three cocktails at a sitting.

We crafted the ultimate weekend trail where we got absolutely hammered on those Dallas BBQ cocktails. Next stop would be the Naked Lunch in SoHo. We'd just stylishly sip on some more cocktails at the Soho Grand Hotel bar. Or doubled down on seeing double at Double Happiness in NoLita. Every once in a while, we'd wrap things up at the skanky The Web in Midtown East. Or take to the high-energy dance floor at Roxy Saturdays which were gay nights at the famous The Roxy. Sundays were sacred and devoted to Sunday hangover brunches. And that was how we rolled in the Big Apple.

Gradually, I was less emotionally dependent on Jai. Most of my time was spent gallivanting about with the gang, we were on an indulgent spree.

8

We Met at The Met

None of my friends in the gang seem to share the same enthusiasm as I do for art, museums, arthouse films, and non-mainstream music.

I have a profound interest in art since young. Won my first art competition when I was five. And growing up with two sisters, I was the lucky recipient of the latest in last season's fashion, not to mention toys that had seen better days and books so old they were practically historical documents. All thanks to my heroic single mom who managed to raise us three girls without a dime from my disappearing act dad.

My possessions could be counted on one hand - two if you count each sock individually - I was a bit of a minimalist, not by choice, but by necessity. Cash flow was more of a trickle, so new things were as rare as a quiet moment in our house. But then, like a light bulb in a dark room, art competitions entered my life. Winning meant more than just ego boosting; it was like a treasure hunt, where the treasure was shiny new things I could call my own - trophies, crayons, paintbrushes, you name it. My sister, Kaylee, had this uncanny ability to sniff out these competitions like a bloodhound on a trail, and she'd march me to these competitions, knowing well my penchant for winning - and for shiny new things.

When I was six, my mom shared some of my artwork with an art school. In my two-toned artwork, I neatly dissected everything into two and they were either crayoned or painted in two different shades of a color. For example, the trunk of a tree would be neatly divided into two columns. The left column would be painted brown and the right column, a darker shade of brown. My split personality in the art world got me accepted into the art school with fees waived. Score.

Left to our devices, Kaylee ended up being my unofficial guardian. My mom was a bit of a serial dater and most weekends, we got a parade of Mom's boyfriends doing the walk of shame past our lunch plates. Those were usually my art class days. I was supposed to be molding my raw talent at 9 AM on Sundays, but instead, I was usually home because Mom was too busy sleeping off her latest romantic escapade. It was messing with my art - my sanctuary, my creative oasis in the desert of domestic chaos - that's where I draw the line with a thick, angry, crimson crayon.

One Sunday, she was snuggled up in bed with a mystery man. Red-faced and fuming, I knew I was about to miss my art class – again. I kungfu-kicked her bedroom door open which startled both their naked butts out of bed. With great bravado, I clambered onto my soapbox, all puffed up with righteous indignity, and hollered at the top of my lungs about my burning desire to attend my art class.

That didn't go down well, I got whacked more times than a piñata. That was the end of my illustrious art school career. From that day forth, a wedge of resentment and hostility lodged itself into my relationship with my mom.

When I was in secondary school, I discovered that words were wings for the imagination. I was penning stories left, right, and center. Entertainment is in my blood, and I realized I could make readers giggle, chuckle or cry. So, I say, first find your passion, and the rest is history. Winning writing competitions became easy to me.

After I quit my Conference Director position, I found myself diving headfirst into the wild world of advertising as a creative copywriter. There, I found myself back into the vibrant realm of creativity, becoming a fanatic of arts, culture, music, and arthouse movies.

When I anchored in the Big Apple, she became a creative playground with unlimited creative offerings. Who needs a job when I had a thirst for drinking up the city's smorgasbord of arts and culture. Mornings and afternoons were mine when Jai was at work.

Boredom became inspiring. It pushed me off my cushy seat to learn and discover through roaming neighborhoods and knocking on the doors of museums like Guggenheim, American Museum of Natural History, Whitney and International Center of Photography. Silence was comforting. I loved quietly passing judgment on all the art and photography exhibitions.

SoHo was my artistic playground. Some days I'd bounce around from art gallery to art gallery. My stomping grounds? Angelika Film Center and Film Forum, the arthouse movie theatres where my movie marathons took place. I'd buy a ticket for a morning movie. Then slip into another hall for a second movie. Then a third. Then a fourth. Not only was I saving enough on tickets to rival any extreme couponer, but I was also binging on movies all day. It was pure, unadulterated joy for me.

The first time I discovered what an "arthouse" film

was, I was standing in front of Film Forum. Back in Singapore, we were all about those popcorn munching, soda slurping blockbusters. Unknown to me, my first arthouse film in Singapore was *Naked Lunch* by David Cronenberg. I was just 15 at the time, I couldn't make sense of the surrealist plot and trippy substance abuse scenes. One of my all-time favorite movies is *The Russian Ark.* I think I first saw it at Film Forum. That movie lit a fire under me and got me all excited again about Russian and Soviet Union history and literature.

Nothing screams "classy" like smuggling a bottle of wine and salmon bagel into a theatre. Why settle for popcorn and soda when you can have a full-on gourmet experience? Jai joined in my movie marathons over weekends but paid for tickets, and he absolutely loved the experience.

Fridays at The Met, short for The Metropolitan Museum, became my weekly ritual. I've rustled up a few fancy facts from Wikipedia, just for you:

- It is the largest art museum in The Americas.
- It ranks eighth on the list of the most-visited art museums in the world.
- Its permanent collection contains over two million works, divided among 17 curatorial departments.

- The main building at 1000 Fifth Avenue, along the Museum Mile on the eastern edge of Central Park on Manhattan's Upper East Side, is by area one of the world's largest art museums.
- The museum's permanent collection consists of works of art from classical and ancient Egypt, paintings and sculptures from nearly all the European Old Masters, and an extensive collection of American and modern art.
- The Met maintains extensive holdings of African, Asian, Oceanian, Byzantine and Islamic art.
- The museum is home to encyclopedic collections of musical instruments, costumes and accessories, as well as antique weapons and armor from around the world.
- Several notable interiors, ranging from 1st-century Rome through modern American design, are installed in its galleries.

The Met is flippin' staggering. It's like The Hermitage in St. Petersburg, which means it cannot be finished in a few days, let alone a day. If you're the sort who goes through everything with a fine-tooth comb like me, weeks aren't going to cut it too. That was why I went to The Met every

Friday and saw a small chunk each time. Plus, they have this symphony that jams out at six in the evening, it's a win-win.

One visit stood out. It was a nail-biting day, and I had intended to explore the Egyptian section, a mind-boggling spectacle of 26,000 objects. We're talking everything from the Paleolithic to the Roman period. Now, this sounds silly to you, but what was even more intimidating to me was the thought of coming face to face with a revived mummy.

Once, I was alone in the Egyptian section at The Penn Museum in Philadelphia. It was on a slow day so you could count the number of folks there on one hand. I was so engrossed in the mummy couture, I didn't even clock the fact that I was flying solo. No guard. No presence. Just me and some otherworldly presence. Suddenly, I bolted for the exit like a cat with its tail on fire. I bet the security guards in the camera room were rolling with laughter and replaying my 'runway' exit on the security cam.

In the Egyptian corner of The Met, I was playing a careful game of red light, green light. I was waiting for some unsuspecting visitors to enter each room, just to make sure I wasn't alone. But then, a spooky presence seemed to be tailing me. "Don't turn around, don't turn around," I chanted to myself like a scared chicken.

"Miss", a voice as smooth as melted chocolate echoed from behind. The presence talked. I swiveled on my heel, my suspicion dial turned up to eleven. "Yes?" Our brown eyes locked. A man, probably in his early 30s, now occupied my field of vision. He was sporting a security guard uniform that looked like it had been borrowed from a guy twice his size. His black hair hung straight and just shy of his shoulders. His face, a gentle canvas of olive hues, was topped off with bangs that could have been my hairstyle's twin. His smile, reaching all the way to his eyes, were deep-set. He was practically radiating sunshine.

Guard: "I thought I'd say hello. Are you OK?"

Me: "Absolutely! Why wouldn't I be?"

Guard: "I see you here every Friday. Alone. I've always wanted to talk to you. What's your name?"

Me: "Kim. You?"

Guard: "I'm Malik. Nice to meet you."

Me: "Nice to meet you too, Malik. Where are you from? I couldn't figure from your accent."

Malik: "I'm Palestinian."

Me: "I'm from Singapore. I moved to the Big Apple a few months ago."

Announcement: "Ladies and gentlemen. The museum will be

closed in ten minutes."

Me: "Looks like I have to go."

Malik: "Can I take you out? I'd like to see you again. Not here. Somewhere else."

Me: "I have a fiancé. I can't date you and won't lead you on."

Malik: "That's OK. I'd still like to see you. Here's my number. Give me a call. Let's arrange something. I would love to hear from you."

Me: "OK. Have a good weekend."

I winked and scooted on out before the mummies decided to stretch their legs. When I got home, I gave Jai the rundown and he just laughed. There was not a single trace of green-eyed monster, as if he was confident his fiancé wouldn't ditch him for a security guard at The Met.

I'd never met a Palestinian before. Sure, I'd seen the clashes on BBC news, but this was a real-life, breathing Palestinian. I was intrigued. Jai must've heard the gears in my head churning away. "Go meet him. He could be a new friend, he said, generously urging his someday-bride-to-be to meet another man.

A few days later, I texted Malik who was really pleased that I got in touch. He invited me for lunch on his upcoming day off, at a Midtown diner.

I strolled in a fashionably ten minutes late to our no-frills, less pressure, definitely-not-a-date diner rendezvous. Spotting Malik at the entrance, he popped up from his chair like a piece of toast from a hyperactive toaster. Seeing him again, I was reminded of his pleasing face and vibe. It was like being wrapped in a warm blanket of calm.

Malik coiled his hair into a tidy tail of pony, showing off his chiseled features. My heart skipped a beat as he was in a suit and tie. The man was the epitome of fashion bravery, rocking a forest green suit with a purple tie. The suit's sleeves were so long, they were practically kissing his knuckles. It was a part sweet, part comedic sight.

He shook my hand and thanked me profusely for meeting him. Then he peeled off his green suit, folded it with the accuracy of an origami master and placed it on the table. Underneath, he sported a shirt as white as fresh snowfall. He sat there, posture rigid, hands and elbows arranged on the table like he was a modern-day Egyptian sphinx.

Over lunch, we became the narrators of our own life stories, each one of us giving a glimpse of our pasts. My mundane life paled in comparison to his show-stopping story. Turns out, he used to be a Palestinian police officer with the Palestinian Civil Police Force and lived in the Old

City of Jerusalem. As he had had enough of the political strife, he decided to start afresh in America, land of the free. With his ambitions set high, he headed for New York and sought political asylum there.

After countless years of waiting, the golden ticket finally arrived – his refugee status. He received it with a solemn nod and a wistful sigh, saying with a twinkle in his eye, "Well, it's no better than being a prisoner, really. I'm stuck in America now." His status had a few limitations. He was not allowed to move in and out of the country at will, which meant he couldn't see his family. But just as he was about to reach the climax of his tale, his cellphone rang.

"Excuse me. I must take this call. It's very important," he said with an air of importance wrapped in a cloak of politeness. I could hear faint screams from the other end. A frantic woman, her voice as high-pitched as a violin in distress, was laying out a saga that I could only imagine. He listened, his face blanker than a sheet of fresh printer paper, responding occasionally in what I could only assume was Arab. I couldn't help but marvel at his tranquility.

Instinctively, I knew something wasn't right. He hung up the phone, a couple of words of goodbye and all, and I found myself trying to decode his blank expression. After a few minutes of silence, he broke the ice. His voice was soft, almost a whisper, "That was my mother. There's an incursion in the West Bank, where my family is now. Everyone is very frightened. My mother just told me she split my family up – my sisters, brothers, their children, my uncles, aunties and their children. She sent them in different directions so they wouldn't be killed at the same time."

Hot tears furiously streamed down my burning cheeks, and I was overwhelmed by a tornado of emotions – anger, sadness, fear and confusion. And yet, there he was, taking it on the chin with calmness.

"Do you mind if I leave now? I am very sorry, but I am going to wait for my family to call. Can I take you out again?" He asked, all manners and politeness, before he footed the bill. It took me years to process the happenings of that peculiar afternoon. I welled up writing this as it was then, and still is, an emotionally loaded moment. I buried it deep under the reams of happy memories I have of New York.

Did I see Malik again? Yes. But, weirdly enough, I didn't want to see him anywhere but the museum. Maybe it was my cowardly way of dealing with the maelstrom of emotions stirred, and the canyon of sadness that I felt. Caught by surprise, I offered no words of consolation to him on that fateful day in the diner, and it acid-stung that I offered nothing. It became a ball and chain of guilt that weighed me down for many years.

Malik knew about my Fridays at The Met. He walked me through sections in the museum if he was on duty. Sometimes he swapped sections with his colleagues to take me through the sections I desired to see.

The last time I saw Malik was at the very provocative photo exhibition by Richard Avedon, one of my most cherished photographers. There was Malik, strolling along with me, explaining that there was more to the pictures sitting pretty on the wall, with their silent yet powerful social and political diatribes.

"You see that picture over there?" Malik pointed to an extremely disturbing close-up of George Wallace, the Governor of Alabama which was taken in November 1963. George Wallace had a piercing look of condescension and utter conceit. "Uh huh," I responded, waiting for a reveal. "Now look across at that picture." He pointed to a black and white picture of the young and hopeful faces of Jerome Smith and Issac Reynolds, two Black student civil rights organizers. Then he explained, "George Wallace was a white supremacist. The placement of the two pictures across each other, creates a powerful spatial dynamic and irony."

It clicked in that moment. The white supremacist faced off the two Black students. That was a powerful spatial play, not described in the museum leaflets or the audio guide.

He took me through a few more exhibits, each one unfolding like a secret chapter in a storybook, adding a whole new dimension to the concept of spatial play. They're permanently etched into the canvas of my mind. Thanks to him, I'll never look at a museum—or anything else, for that matter—the same way again.

I finally landed a job which sounded the death knell for my Fridays at The Met. Malik often wanders into my thoughts, and I find myself wondering how he's faring.

Whenever I see television reports depicting the violent clashes between Israelis and Palestinians, I can't help but think about Malik's family and the numerous innocent people, plunged into the whirlpool of relentless violence. The senselessness of it all is heart-wrenching.

On October 7, 2023, at around 6:30 am, Hamas launched a surprise incursion into Israel. The world reeled in shock. I pray for all victims, Israeli and Palestinian. I hope the conflict will end in my lifetime.

9

Bridge and Tunnel

So, there we were, another entertaining night under our belts, lined up like a parade of giggling misfits making our tipsy trek to the infamous Naked Lunch. This was a small, crowded and cozy bar a few blocks away from the loft. Music there was always good, and the crowds were always wild. It was one of those good-times-guaranteed spots.

One of the troop decided to bring along a buddy, a fresh face in our well-worn crew. He wasn't familiar with our usual haunts, so he shot a query, "Naked Lunch? The one full of bridge and tunnel peeps?" I asked what that meant as I wasn't privy to the term. He looked at me, a grin spreading across his face, and explained that 'bridge and tunnel' was the tag they slapped on folks from New Jersey.

Not content with the rather limited explanation and sensing there was more to the term, I looked it up the next day. Here's 'bridge and tunnel', as defined by the mighty Wikipedia:

"Bridge and Tunnel (often abbreviated B&T or BNT) is a term – often used pejoratively – to describe people who live in communities surrounding the island of Manhattan in New York City, and commute to it for work or entertainment. It refers to the fact that vehicular travel to the island of Manhattan requires passing over a bridge or through a tunnel. Some use it to describe residents of the other four boroughs of New York City – Brooklyn, Queens, the Bronx, and Staten Island – but it typically refers to those who travel into the city from outside the area served by the New York City Subway (thus by car), including the Hudson Valley, New Jersey, Connecticut, and Long Island."

Just like that, my New York lexicon was one phrase richer. What the guy meant by 'bridge and tunnel peeps' were the enthusiastic hordes who weaved through the labyrinth of bridges and tunnels, to indulge in the enticing allure of Manhattan's nightlife.

At our Sunday ritual, the post-Saturday-night-fever brunch at our go-to joint, The Cupping Room, I gingerly nudged the topic into our conversation. Sud, in between delicately cutting his home fries and elegantly forking them into his mouth, shed light on the term further.

Sud: "Have you seen *The Sopranos*?"

Me: "The mafia series?"

Sud: "Yeah. The one with James Gandolfini."

Me: "Hmm... I'm not following the series, but I know what you're talking about."

Sud: "Do you remember how they were dressed? Matching tracksuits and tacky outfits?"

Me: "Oh yes."

Sud: "The small-town mentality?"

Me: "Uh huh."

Sud: "That's bridge and tunnel for you."

That social stigma clung to me tight, forever. I wasn't always this judgmental, but somehow, I found myself unconsciously categorizing people. Whether they were colleagues (when I had finally managed to snag a job), new friends, casual acquaintances, or even the unsuspecting strangers I passed on the streets - they all went through my unpatented B&T filter. The fine people from New Jersey had the misfortune of being on the lowest rung of this B&T ladder. As Kaylee lived in New Jersey, it started a decade-long internal conflict.

Kaylee found herself in hot pursuit of the ever-elusive American dream in her early 30s. She was kicked out of our dysfunctional home at 19. My mom had a baby with her boyfriend then and no knew she'd been expecting, let alone given birth. The day mom waltzed in, newborn in tow, Kaylee was none the wiser. She went about her day as usual, unaware of the new addition to our already packed circus. She startled the sensitive newborn when she closed the door. And just like that, Kaylee was exiled to live with my horrible aunt. This joyous arrangement lasted a few months until Kaylee, finished university.

A wounded warrior and a gritty fighter who wouldn't quit when the going gets tough, Kaylee got herself a job, rented an apartment, found herself a boyfriend and lived with him for over a decade. But one fateful morning, he did the unthinkable. He packed his tiny backpack and walked out the door, never to return. He left her a note. In it, he explained that Kaylee's abusive ways were driving him up the wall and he could no longer share his life with her.

Kaylee hit rock bottom and was beside herself with rage for a year. Usually introverted and a total homebody, she became a bar-hopping social butterfly overnight. She met Brad, an American tourist visiting Singapore, at one of the bars. She took a leap of faith, packing her suitcase with her few precious possessions that still sparked joy. Convinced that there was no turning back, she got herself a one-way ticket and headed to Philadelphia, where the promise of a new life with Brad awaited. She left everything unhappy in the dust behind and never, ever looked back.

With their bags packed and hearts heavy, Brad and Kaylee set their sights on the bustling suburbia of Edison, New Jersey. It was just a hop, skip, and a tunnel away from SoHo. Nestled right at the end of the Holland Tunnel, was our SoHo loft. Jai and I had a running gag that we were the light at the end of the Holland Tunnel.

I used to make the solitary trek by train to Edison just to see them. Jai, on the other hand, wouldn't go near New Jersey. It wasn't because he was hung up on the B&T tag, but he simply couldn't stand being in their company. Brad, a Republican and ultra conservative, had a small-town mentality which drove Jai up the wall. Then there was the constant bickering between Brad and Kaylee. You could say it was a bit prickly to be around them.

Not your ordinary sisterhood, ours was a bond forged in the fires of mom's hot temper. Kaylee, the ever so brave one, would often find herself on the receiving end of mom's fury. Sometimes she was hit so bad, I had to bring her to our family doctor who once begged us to go to the police. Despite the pain and the tears, she refused to split up our dynamic duo as she was afraid we'd end up in different foster homes.

Forget about sibling rivalry. It was sibling enmity with my middle sister Kyra. She was not just a snitch, but a full-blown double agent in the sibling warfare. She was a regular tattletale, always ratting out poor Kaylee to our mom. I dug deep in the trenches with Kaylee as I felt I had a duty to protect her and keep the connection going, even though we are as different as day and night.

An extreme introvert, Kaylee has a small circle of friends. I was her de facto family, as she had cut everyone else off. Back then, her social calendar consisted of Brad, the gang, and me. At those wild loft parties we used to throw, there was Kaylee, huddled up in a corner, clinging onto a Coke like it was a lifebelt. Socializing and partying wasn't up her alley. But there she was, sticking it out, pretty much like I would for her.

Brad and Kaylee became bridge and tunnel people, strictly by definition. Fast forward ten years, with their epic relocation to Pennsylvania, post my departure from New York, I was finally snapped out of my tunnel vision.

10

Intercourse. Blue ball. Bird-in-hand.

Intercourse, Blue Ball and Bird-in-Hand may sound like porn shop names to me, but they are charmingly peculiar town names in the heart of Lancaster County, Pennsylvania. I had a field day of chuckles when Kaylee drove us there for my first dip in Amish culture.

Kaylee's love for long drives and my fondness for quirky adventures complemented each other. I, the hapless non-driver, found a perfect road trip companion in Kaylee. No matter where our whims pointed us, she was always game to navigate us there. Our escapades took us to many fascinating places, but it was our Amish trip that found a permanent spot in our collective memory.

As we rolled into Lancaster County, we were greeted with the soothing greens of the rolling hills and countryside. Laundry lines filled with dark, solid-colored clothes flapping wildly and freely in the wind, against the backdrop of a horizon of bountiful fields and farmlands.

Lancaster County has the oldest Amish communities in the country. Take a stroll into their historic downtown, and you'll see well-preserved 18th and 19th century architecture. The Amish remains the biggest tourist attraction with their simple and rural lifestyles. A sight for sore, city-tired eyes.

Their discerning use of technology in today's world of advanced technology is unfathomable. Some Amish progressives use torchlights, radios and telephones. Now on the other side of the fence, the conservatives avoid electricity use – preferring batteries and generators over the public grid. The Amish community isolate themselves and keep interactions with the outside world minimal, yet they remain utterly fascinating to us.

After an exhausting journey on the road, Kaylee and I found ourselves pulling into a gas station to refuel both the car and ourselves. We ambled into the convenience store in search of refreshments. She snagged a few bags of chips and bottles of juice, making her way to the cashier.

Meanwhile, my attention was magnetically pulled, no pun intended, towards a metal wall adorned with a plethora of magnets. I, being the sentimental fool that I am, had taken up the hobby of collecting magnets of places visited. They were stuck on my fridge as keepsakes.

My eyes were drawn to a peculiar metallic magnet. It bore the names of towns that made me blush - Intercourse, Blue Ball, and Bird-in-Hand. I couldn't help but chuckle at the absurdity and plucked it off the wall for a closer look.

The cashier caught my confused expression and offered an explanation, "These are names of towns here in Lancaster." He then followed up with a rhetorical question, "Don't they sound strange to you?" I stared at the town names etched on the magnet in incredulity. How on earth did such a conservative, religious county end up with such filthy town names?

Kaylee prodded me in my ribs with the enthusiasm of a child who had just spotted a candy store. "Look over there," she stage-whispered, pointing to a small selection of cakes delicately placed on antique stands and protected like treasures under glass lids. "They're Amish and delish. The Amish sure know how to bake," she said, her eyes wide and gleaming with mischief.

I followed her pointed finger to the neat hand-written labels that hung in front of each cake. 'Carrot cake', 'Apple fritter bread', and 'Whoopie pie'. What on earth is a whoopie pie? I thought to myself as I paid for the magnet that would soon become a prized memento.

Kaylee, who was spellbound by all things Amish, then droned on about the 1985 movie *Witness,* starring Harrison Ford. Filmed in the heart of Lancaster County, the plot was simple enough - Ford was a cop tasked with protecting an Amish woman and her son after he had witnessed a brutal murder. Ford's character had to somehow blend in with the Amish community while keeping a 24/7 watch over his charges. Good luck with that.

Kaylee's words tumbled to a halt. "Lee!" she hollered. That's my pet name my family slapped on me. "Look! An Amish buggy!" She flitted from the storefront window to the outside, in a blink of an eye. I peered out of the window. There was Kaylee, armed with her digital camera, clicking away with unabashed enthusiasm. The object of her photographic fervor? A horse-drawn Amish buggy parked at the gas station, right next to a line of shiny modern cars.

A man, as pale as the moonlight, with a beard so long, stepped out of a carriage. He was dressed in a peculiar ensemble, a black hat perched on his head, and a light blue long-sleeved shirt neatly tucked into his black trousers. Following him, a woman dressed head to toe in black swiftly descended from the carriage. A black bonnet sat atop her head. Her appearance stoked Kaylee even more as she blindsided the pair with an onslaught of photographs.

So, there I was, barreling towards Kaylee to snatch the camera from her mischievous hands. As I managed to do just that, I turned to the Amish couple, and stammered out an apology. The tomfoolery was unexpected and out of character for Kaylee.

Returning to our dusty, four-wheeled haven, I slipped into the role of the elderly sister. "That was super embarrassing. Don't do that again!" Kaylee took the sting out of my words with giggles. That was our first and last encounter with the Amish community.

We had more road trips lined up. Kaylee drove us to Princeton, in New Jersey where the biggest draw is the prestigious Princeton University. We did our quiet walk through the picturesque campus grounds, ventured further afield into the charming historic surroundings and posed for pictures at Albert Einstein's rather underwhelming, but true to his character house at 112 Mercer Street.

Bent on covering more campus grounds because of the easy-going vibes, we drove to Massachusetts University of Technology in Cambridge. If we couldn't make the cut at these prestigious universities, the least we could do was to soak up the campus spirit. We also satisfied my appetite for boundary-pushing robotics and innovation at MIT Museum.

We moved from land to shore, the 141-mile Atlantic coastline of Jersey Shore specifically, to join sun devotees and boardwalk strollers at Cape May, Ocean City and Atlantic City. At Caesars Casino, I had a sudden realization that I had left my wallet at home. Kaylee refused to lend me money for the slot machines due to her disdain for gambling. We did what most do at Casinos - load up on food at the buffet.

Road trips were how Kaylee and I bonded as adults. The change in scenery from Singapore to the US, New York or New Jersey to the towns we visited redefined our sisterhood. We explored new comfort zones, outside the discomfort zones of our abusive childhood in Singapore. At my lowest points in New York, Kaylee took me on therapeutic road trips. Sometimes you need to skip out of town, far away from the Big Apple madness and hit reset.

I'd like to think Kaylee found the road trips curative too. On our journeys, she shared her unhappiness in her marriage. She was conflicted between two journeys in her marriage – to stay or to leave. The more journeys we went on, the closer she came to the reconciliation that there was only one journey for her – to stay.

11

Polish Mystery

Out of all the outlandish experiences I've had the pleasure to encounter in New York, the 'Polish mystery' takes the cake.

For the sake of those who might not be familiar with the term 'Apartment Superintendent', or 'Super', they are property or residential managers who oversee maintenance, upkeep, and repairs in the apartment. You'll often find them living either close to the apartment or right in the apartment itself, usually on the ground floor or in the basement. They often live there rent-free or at a reduced rate. Apart from the housing benefits, they might also receive a wage. Supers are the liaisons between the tenants and the landlord.

Our Polish Super, Jacek, was a live-in easy-going character. Age had caught up with him, landing him in his 50s, but it had done nothing to tame his wild, dirty blonde hair. His attire was always a pair of grubby overalls that seemed to have a lifelong partnership with dirt. His smile? A bit on the unconventional side, thanks to a couple of missing teeth, which made pronunciations hard for him. Deciphering his English, layered thick with Polish accent was even harder.

Jacek lived in the basement with his wife, Beata, and their son, Marcin. Beata, a woman of hearty girth, sported a mane of untamed dirty blonde waves that framed her stony, and hardened face. She was the type who wouldn't even crack a smile if someone slipped on a banana peel. She hardly spoke. And when she did, her words were in Polish.

Young Marcin, a strapping guy in his early 20s was a clean-shaven, muscular lad who was neither good looking nor ugly. As an in-betweener, he didn't stand out in a crowd. Often dressed in military green attire, you might think you've stumbled upon a neo-Nazi if you passed him on the street. Like his parents, he was a bit of a hermit. Bump into him in the hallway and he'd toss you a friendly hello.

Jacek and Beata had a friend Jakub, who helped with the occasional odd jobs. Jakub was pushing 60, short, petite and sported a head full of shiny silver curls. Slap a pair of round-rimmed glasses on him and you've got a professor moonlighting as a handyman. Jakub didn't exactly live in our apartment, but he might as well have with the amount of time he spent at Jacek's when he wasn't out fixing something.

Their pastime? Card playing and drinking. And when

I say drinking, I mean copious amounts of drinking by East European standards. Sometimes they'd get so tipsy, they'd be causing a din. Since they were squirreled away in the basement, residents took to turning a blind eye to them.

Jacek was nowhere to be seen for a while. The apartment was starting to look like a junkyard with a backlog of repairs. We were almost convinced that he had skipped out of town. One day, we bumped into Jakub in the laundry room. Adjusting his glasses like a bewildered owl, he nonchalantly dropped the bombshell that Jacek was hospitalized. His fondness for drinking landed him with cirrhosis.

A month later, there was Jacek, back at our apartment, looking like he'd been shrunk in the wash. He was doing some DIY in our loft. When we asked how he was doing, he told us he'd been diagnosed with cirrhosis and wasn't allowed to drink anymore. His face was a picture of pure misery.

Quiet became the new norm in the basement when Jacek decided to stick to his will. But alas, only a month later, the merriments once again echoed down the basement hallway. It appeared that bottles won the battle over his diluted will.

One late evening, the most peculiar happened. Jacek, Beata and Jakub were engaged in their usual marathon of cards and a heavy round of drinking. Suddenly, Jacek collapsed onto the table. Jakub and Beata, not even batting an eyelid, assumed he had just reached his liquor limit a bit earlier than usual. So, they just shrugged, and carried on with their game. Then, Beata also face-planted onto the table. Jakub, now alone, left them on the table and stumbled off home. Here's the shocker. It turns out Jacek and Beata died of alcohol poisoning that night.

Just when you thought that was jaw-dropping, there was another turn of the screw to the Polish mystery. That same night, Marcin was out on the town, painting Brooklyn red with his friends. He got himself stabbed.

When the residents heard the news the next day, we were left bereft of words. It was an unbelievable triple tragedy. Poor Marcin survived the stabbing, but had to evict as we had a new Super moving in. How's that for insult to injury. When it comes to empathy, New York City is certainly short of it.

12

Lights, Camera, Action!

I'm a film buff who devours both popcorn flicks and fancy-pants arthouse productions. I'm hopelessly hooked on a few series, just like every other breathing human being. Living in SoHo fanned the flames of my passion for movie magic and series mania even more.

When it came to cheap and cheerful eats in SoHo, our top choices were Moondance Diner, Reuben's Empanadas, Lupe's East LA Kitchen and Broome Street Bar.

Moondance Diner was basically our second home, snugly tucked away at the corner of Grand Street and the Avenue of the Americas, just a stone's throw from our SoHo loft. This was our favorite diner where we nursed our hangovers with greasy fry-ups, ate our Sunday brunches, read our New York Times over filtered coffee, doggy-bagged our hurried weekday dinner and sobered up after a long night of drinking. The neighborhood diner attracted a hodge-podge of diners ranging from creative and artistic types to neighbors, wide-eyed tourists and wearied commuters who had just survived the Holland Tunnel.

The shiny-chromed, retro diner was an eyecatcher in the street. This place had a massive yellow crescent on top that was fluorescent lit at night. It boasted a sign that read 'Moondance', but with all those sequins, it looked more like 'Moonprance'. It stood out in the unassuming industrial-looking tail-end of SoHo. The diner was snugly fit into an old railway car, making the interior crammed. A short bar counter was fronted by metallic highchairs that looked like they were stolen from a 1950s sci-fi movie set. A short row of tables offered off-the-counter seats.

Moondance Diner wasn't just another friendly neighborhood diner. It was the Hollywood of diners, a real A-lister. Monica Gellar worked as a waitress here in *Friends*. So did Mary Jane in *Spiderman*. Tourists and star-struck fans soon made a beeline for the diner.

This one morning, I found myself at the diner, my nose practically buried in the opened pages of New York Times. Mornings were usually quiet with lone diners engrossed in their morning reads, typing away at their next big screenplay, or penning down ideas for their next novel, all while nursing a cup of strong joe. Once I'd had enough of the

Times' tales, I strutted across the joint for the shiny chrome exit and flung the door open.

"CUT!" echoed through the air and I jumped out of my skin. Without realizing, I had strolled straight into the middle of a TV show being filmed. In my confusion, I spotted a clapperboard being hoisted, with *CSI New York* written on it. I didn't notice who the actors were, the episode number on the clapperboard or any other pertinent details. I simply bolted in embarrassment. Did my walk disrupt their crime-solving scene? Will I make a guest appearance on CSI New York? What episode will forever immortalize my moment of embarrassment? Unfortunately, those answers remain as unsolved as a cold case.

The closure of the notable diner in 2007 was so newsworthy that it made headlines in the New York Times, CNBC, and even BBC. Years later, like a phoenix rising from the ashes, it made a comeback. The railway car from the diner got a second shot at fame. Did you see Netflix film *Tick Tick... Boom!*? Some scenes were shot in that very railway car, that was stashed somewhere, off-location in SoHo. And here's a fun fact: Jonathan Larson, the guy who wrote *Rent*, was a weekend waiter here for a whole decade. I wondered if he ever waited on me.

Who could forget that steamy scene between Diane Lane and hunky Olivier Martinez in the 2002 flick, *Unfaithful?* Filmed in the bathroom of Café Noir, the former hotspot on 32 Grand and Thompson Street. Not that I'm stalking or anything, but it was just a stone's throw away from the Varick loft. The gang got so tired of me going on and on about recreating that saucy scene with Olivier, probably the only person on earth who could get you to stray from Richard Gere.

Over the years, I've learned to do the set-sidestepping samba, rather than the faceplant foxtrot into them. SoHo burst at her seams with productions. When the big guns of the movie world rolled into town, you'd see celebrity trailers parked up, hogging the cobbled streets. Not to mention, the elaborate catering. And during those teeth-chattering winters, it was as cozy as a kitten in a mitten watching the crew huddle over their steaming cups of joe in the bustling cobbled streets.

Production lightings are like the divas of the film set - always wanting to be the first one set up, taking up all the space, and demanding all the attention. I know this as I did shoots in advertising agencies. You wouldn't believe it, but it often took weeks to set up the lighting on the hustling, bustling streets of SoHo. We're talking big productions here.

And the funny thing is, when you're watching the scene, you don't even notice the lights.

Keeping up with appearances was and still is a major theme in SoHo. I learned to dress to the nines when performing menial tasks such as buying olives from the corner store. You never knew when a surprise film crew might pop up or when you'd bump into a celeb. I've had casual run-ins with the likes of William Dafoe and Kevin Bacon. Even bumped into Kevin's wife, Kyra Sedgwick, and the fabulous Carrie Bradshaw. And let's not forget ogling at Denzel Washington getting jacked at our local gym. He was getting ripped for his role in *The Manchurian Candidate*.

Fast forward a few years and there I was, living the high life with my own loft on West Broadway, nestled snugly between Broome and Grand Street. I spotted Naomi Campbell at the local watering hole. She was sipping on a glass of wine, all by her lonesome, without a single tantrum in sight.

There was one celebrity Kaylee and I almost dined with, at a cozy French brasserie snuggled between Thompson Street and Sixth Avenue on Canal Street. It was a quiet evening, and the dimly lit brasserie was soon lit up by a star.

Britney Spears strolled in, without airs, flanked by her bodyguard. She nabbed a table in the corner, all by her lonesome, while he stood guard a few feet away, probably fantasizing about a juicy steak. She exuded great loneliness and emptiness and gave off this whole "woe is me" vibe. I was as starstruck as a deer in headlights, but I got the hint that she craved her privacy and wanted nothing more than to claim her personal space.

Kaylee and I had all these grand plans on how to introduce ourselves. We thought about throwing a glass her way and belting out Britney Spears' "Hit me baby one more time". Okay, maybe not the best idea - especially considering her bodyguard looked like the bloodletting sort. We didn't dare move more than an inch.

I've always been gob smacked, by the fact that I hung my hat in a neighborhood that's as star-studded as a planetarium show. Rubbing elbows with famous celebs in SoHo is like having extra sprinkles on my ice cream sundae of life. All I want to know, is if I ever photobombed an episode of CSI New York.

13

Writing

After a year of hedonism and cultural immersion, I decided to head back to school and pursue a Masters degree in... well, something. I already had a Bachelor of Arts and Social Sciences under my belt, with specializations in Sociology and European Studies. For dessert, I took on some side modules like Literature, American Film, and Social Work. Tellingly, I have diverse interests. I like to think that my university years were like an all-you-can-eat buffet of knowledge.

The MFA Program in Creative Writing at New York University caught my eye. I love writing, you see. I mean, I write for work as a Copywriter, but I also write for kicks. However, the requirements for the program were tedious. They wanted testimonials from my former professors. Easy peasy, I thought. I'll just hit up my old professors from my alma mater in Singapore. But alas, they moved on to greener pastures in other countries. Of course, this was before the era of Facebook, Instagram, or LinkedIn. Trying to find them was like trying to find a needle in a haystack.

So, in the end, I picked a Creative Writing course taught by the award-winning playwright, Karen Malpede, at The Graduate School and University Center of the City University of New York. CUNY Graduate Center for short. Handy enough, it was nestled right between 34th and 35th Streets on Fifth Avenue. No sweat for my commuting game.

There I was - back in the classroom with my belly full of butterflies, feeling like a kindergartner on their first day. We all took turns introducing ourselves and explaining why we had signed up for the creative writing class. The reasons were mostly cookie-cutter. That is, until we got to a lady in the middle of the room.

Diagnosed with severe ADHD, short for Attention-deficit / hyperactivity disorder, she wanted to take the course as a personal gauntlet. Not at all fitting the student mold, she seemed more of a bored housewife who took up writing over knitting. I yearned to hear her story.

I introduced myself to her after the class ended. We were vibing, and I decided to bring up her ADHD. She froze mid-sentence, almost like someone had hit the pause button. Her eyes darted to the ground, and you could cut the awkwardness with a knife. And then, without uttering a single word, she spun around and walked away. Let's just say, it was the most severe case of ADHD and acute inattentiveness I'd ever seen.

On a side note, I wonder if you're a writer. Or maybe you're already a sprouting little wordsmith. Stephen King's book "On Writing: A Memoir of the Craft" has more knockout tips than a boxing match. If you think I'm some kind of horror aficionado, I'll have you know that I've never so much as glanced at a single page of a horror book or peeked through my fingers at a horror movie. Horror is a genre I avoid.

An inspiring tip, amongst a litany of others from Karen Malpede, was to 'drop in' on seemingly ordinary, banal and inane conversations at diners, in the streets, at the park or frankly, wherever your nosy self wanders off to. Astonishingly, those talks are like a gold mine for inspiration. I found it useful and was amazed by the snippets of conversation I 'accidentally' eavesdropped on at the Moondance Diner, my occasional writing spot.

Another wisdom I've gleaned from the world of fictional writing, was that we're the mere conduits of the unfolding story and character developments. Don't script characters into being. Allow them into being. Hard to explain this one as you need to have a feel for it. Words don't do the advice justice.

As part of the writing course, we were assigned the Herculean task of penning a book. I nearly drank myself to ruin during this literary journey. As an inveterate social drinker, I drank copiously at parties, bars and clubs with the gang. Admittedly, bottles emptied fast when I penned my book, *The Soviet Dream*. Back then, I was practically head over heels for everything East European - history, literature, and the infamous Russian gulag.

I won't write a parallel story here but, in a nutshell, the book was about four Russian teenagers who were incarcerated in a small prison cell at a Russian gulag. Each boy personified a famous Russian political figure, except for the fourth boy, who was your everyday Russian proletariat.

First up, we have Nilats, Stalin spelt backwards. In the gulag for petty crimes, he mirrored Stalin and took on Stalin's views, but through the naïve lens of a teenager. Then we've got Alexei, who was Lenin in the making with similar ideologies. Finally, there's Konstantin, doing his best Trotsky impression. Both were wrongfully convicted.

The confined space and reduced mobility in the gulag surprisingly sparked their imaginations, allowing it to soar to incredible heights. Interestingly enough, some of the most powerful literature ever created, was written by former Soviet political prisoners in shackles.

I resurrected the old bitter rivalry between Stalin and Lenin. Short of killing each other, the conversations were filled with rich contrasting perspectives. The views of the proletariat were constantly being shaped and reshaped, influenced by the strength of the arguments put forth by the other three characters. The narrative provided the only platform where all four characters could engage in free debate, as life couldn't possibly mimic art, if Stalin, Lenin and Trotsky were alive.

To truly dive deep into the psyche of my characters, I found myself reaching for a bottle. My creative juices flowed best at nine in the evenings. I would start with a few glasses of chilled vodka tonic, transitioning to neat vodka when Jai called it a night at 11 P.M. I would drink until I reached a state of mental oblivion, but still inconceivably functioned. It reminds me of F. Scott Fitzgerald's words, "First you take a drink, then the drink takes a drink, then the drink takes you."

That was when the fun started. I felt like a conduit for character developments. As I indulged in more drinks, my creativity seemed to expand, leading to unexpected character evolutions. Each night was spent in a somewhat intoxicated state, as I strived to keep pace with the progressing narratives.

Despite this unconventional method, I found myself eagerly anticipating the next morning, where I would read the previous night's work whilst nursing a hangover that felt as large as China itself. Oddly, I had no memory of penning those words. It was truly astonishing to watch how the story unraveled and how the characters seemed to take on lives of their own.

My poor liver wasn't the only thing taking a hit from my actions; our apartment was suffering as well. My loss of control was leading to some messy incidents, where I'd flail about, knocking things over in the process. Jai was a heavy sleeper, so would sleep right through the noise. But each morning, he would wake up to a battlefield – broken lamps, shards of glass on the floor, chairs tossed about, and curtains torn down. Justifiably incensed, he issued an ultimatum to stop drinking.

So, there I was, putting an end to both drinking and writing. In my mind, the two were inseparable. I'm not saying I support Bukowski's habit of drinking excessively while writing, but I noticed a derailment in my inspiration when I quit drinking. At a certain point, my writing course came to an end, but my book didn't. There was never a definite end, a closure to my story.

I mustered all my willpower and began working on my second contemporary book from scratch, titled "Chain." This emotionally intense tale revolves around a unique concept; a reversed daisy chain of individuals who've been victims of violence. The narrative begins with a victim whose life tragically ends, and through a series of carriers, I traced the cycle of violence back to its origin. The underlying premise is that violence, like a contagious disease, spreads from one person to another, only stopping when a life is lost. It also explores the notion that we all harbor seeds of violence within us and, without realizing it, pass them onto others.

I was inspired by the generational violence that persisted in my family - my mom suffered abuse, treated poorly by my dad and his mom. We unwillingly turned into her victims and this cycle of abuse pushed us to mistreat others. Without emptying the bottles, I was on a downhill slide and hit pause.

Disclaimer. I couldn't be more sober when I wrote this memoir. I established a disciplined rigor to write early in the morning to avoid tippling and managed to work around my son's school, rugby, and aviation school schedule.

Astonishingly, I completed this book, hitting the milestone of 63,000 words, in nearly five weeks. Finally, I've reached the finish line without intoxicants and successfully broke the habit I held for two decades. I'll drink to that.

14

Chapter Two – Two Became One

I finally ended my engagement to Jai and kicked off the sequel of my New York saga - "Single in the City". The break up was on the cards when we arrived, for reasons too lengthy to deep dive into. Nonetheless, I'll give you the broad strokes.

A few months before I scarpered off to New York, my buddy was hospitalized in Singapore with malignant brain tumor. During one of my visits, I let it slip that I was having second thoughts about tying the knot with Jai. Her condition took a nosedive, and before you know it, she slipped into a coma and never gained consciousness. Her devastated parents made a gut-wrenching call to turn off her life support, accepting that was the end of the line for her. Her death tore at me and I'll forever remember her parting words of wisdom - "Follow your heart". Everyone else, in their well-meaning manner, was prodding me to stick with the relationship.

After her funeral, I decided to head to Cambodia for a

volunteer stint at an NGO. I was on a mission to find meaning and purpose. There I was, diving headfirst into an outreach program to get street kids off the streets. There, in the midst of all the craziness, I found myself once again pondering over the great breakup. Maybe a new life in New York could change my mind, I persuaded myself.

Distraction is the mother of all escapes. New adventures awaited when I hit the Big Apple, and I bought time to further delay decision making. The greatest escape came in the form of a solo backpacking trip in the South of France, Switzerland and Austria. I leaped off a train in Liechtenstein. The train was nonchalantly chugging from Zurich to Salzburg, completely oblivious to the tiny principality's existence. But I decided to make an unplanned pit stop. After months of living out of a backpack, I traveled with wanton abandon, in favor of risk takings.

At some point, I was forced to confront the feelings I was trying to escape from. Your heart and mind speak aloud when in solitude. They reasoned in unison that it was only fair to Jai if I ended the engagement. Our happily ever after was looking more like a happily never after. We made great friends, but the romance had fizzled. If I loved him, I must let him go, so he had a shot at finding a more fitting soul mate.

When my mindset shifted, a tidal wave of guilt gushed in. I felt deeply sorry that I had disappeared on him while on the road. I went completely off the grid. He was aware that I was backpacking solo, but I never shared that it was also a journey of soul searching. Selfishly, I relished my unbridled freedom at the expense of his suffering. It might not have been the fairest thing, but it felt necessary at the time.

Two months flew by and there I was, heading back to the Big Apple. I kept my return a surprise, didn't really tell anyone. I'd been missing my life there - the friends I had made, the lively rhythm of the city, my cozy loft, the familiar neighborhood, and of course, Jai. The guilt I had been harboring towards him had grown so immense, I couldn't wait to offload. I felt as trapped as a ship in a bottle, yearning for a release.

When I had swung open the door to our cozy loft, a wave of tranquility washed over me as I was greeted by the familiar sight of our cherished furniture. My gaze was drawn to an intriguing mound of gifts nestled in the far-right corner of the loft, right where our comfy daybed resided. Among the heap, I noticed bags from Victoria's Secret, teeming with beautifully wrapped merchandise, along with other assorted parcels. Not knowing who these surprise packages were meant for, I decided it was best to leave them untouched in their snug corner.

In the evening, Jai trudged his way home from yet another monotonous day at work. He was taken aback when he saw me, but then he hugged and kissed me so tightly, it felt like he was squeezing the last bit of toothpaste from a tube. I sat him down and began to share my travel stories – some mundane and others far-fetched. He then pointed out the pile of presents that had accumulated, explaining that he had bought me a gift for each week I was gone. My feelings of guilt started to pile up just as high as the presents. Gathering all the courage I could, I ended our relationship.

We both collapsed onto the daybed, turned on the waterworks, and practically drained the reservoir that was our tear ducts. He didn't want to end us, but he respected my final verdict. We embraced and took a rollercoaster ride down memory lane, going over the ups and downs of our time together. Time took leave as we sat there enveloped by the darkness when the sun dipped.

I finally felt unknotted with a sunny optimism for the next chapter. He felt empty and abandoned. We decided to remain good friends, come what may.

Chapter two was an addictive page turner with the

craziest experiences I've ever had. When two became one, it became one hell of a ride with a blend of highs and lows, with test curveballs constantly thrown at me.

15

Straight Dancer in a Gay Club

Single, footloose and fancy free? If the world is your oyster, the Big Apple is your aphrodisiac center. Whilst *Sex and the City* was booming in popularity on screens, the gang was running our own crazy Asian LG, without the BTQ+, version of it in parallel. According to the gang, I was a cocktail of Samantha Jones and Carrie Bradshaw - twice the fun, double the drama.

Nobody in the gang was surprised when I called the engagement off. Tim already knew, because I spilled my beans to him. Every single one of us was, well, single. Vinny and Thaddeus called it quits too. Finally, I was inducted into the singles club and that was when the wild fun began.

First stop of debauchery – The Web. Nestled between Madison and Park Avenue on 58th Street, this was my initiatory visit to the seedy and skanky gay club. Upon entry, we were immediately ensnared in a sweaty, pulsing mass of humanity. We were a sardine can of shirtless, chiseled muscle

Mary's, all jostling and jiving their way either to or from the bar. Drinks were splashing from every direction. We were caught in a tropical storm of cocktails, making it a very wet and sticky affair of the unpleasant kind.

Faces disappeared fast. The only source of light was a shy red glow, doing a terrible job at its one task. Dance music boomed deafeningly, making conversations impossible. Clearly, the club wasn't designed for talking, it was purely for close-up checking out and hooking up.

We formed a human chain and wriggled our way through the crowd. Tim led us on a magical mystery tour to the stage. There before us were some of the beefiest beefcakes you've ever seen, dressed in tiny shorts. My eyes nearly dilated out of my sockets. What in the world was this? The stage was like a cross between a playground and a maximum-security prison. Poles were being climbed, cages were being wriggled in and out of. My innocent eyes were trying to keep up with the action.

"Kimmie! Stuff these into his pants!" Tim snapped me out of my trance and catapulted me back into the real world. He handed me a fistful of crumpled dollar bills. My eyes darted to the dancers' bulked-up crotches, already jam-packed with dollar bills. Oh, I get it. I sidled up to the nearest gyrating hunk, one of many in the, pardon the pun, web of choices. This one was a real treat, all bronzed muscles, blonde hair, and a chest so shiny and smooth.

Right there, at his feet and mercy, I gawked up at him like a sex-starved, desperate housewife while he gyrated sensually. His eyes spotted the green bucks, and he knew the drill. He descended, thrusted his crotch towards my face, missing my tiny Asian nose by half an inch. Cross-eyed, I frantically and nervously stuffed the wad of dollar bills into his tiny shorts. Once satiated by the paltry deposit, he backed off and launched into a sexy repertoire for my eyes only. Well, at least that's what I told myself.

I worshipped his every tantalizing move and could hear Tim, Sud, Vinny and Claire chanting wildly behind, "Go Kimmie!". What happened next ripped the rug from under my feet. The guy dropped to his knees and suddenly, it was an eye-to-eye situation. His striking face and palpable charisma reduced me to pulp. He managed to hoist his voice over the booming basslines, "What are you doing in thirty minutes?" I shrugged innocently. "I finish my shift in 30 minutes. Meet me at the bar," he instructed.

I was left with my jaw on the floor. He popped up in a jiffy, swung around that pole like a top-notch gymnast, and parked himself on it cross-legged. Twisting back to my crew, their shrieks filled the air, "What did he say?!"

Me: "He asked me to meet him at the bar in half an hour."

Tim: "Oh my God, Kimmie! He is so hot!"

Me: "But he is gay!"

Sud and Tim: "No! He is straight!"

Me: "I don't understand!"

My mind was in short circuit at this point.

Me: "Isn't this a gay club? Isn't everyone gay?"

Tim: "He is straight. He is NOT gay. He is hot and he wants a piece of you! GO MEET HIM!"

Everyone bobbed their heads in excitement. Tim smiled like a Cheshire cat on speed, which he always does.

Half an hour later, I found myself face to face with the dancer at the bar, just like he'd instructed. I wasn't sure what to expect, but I sure wasn't prepared for what I saw. He glided over to me, like he'd just stepped out of a perfume commercial. He was wearing a white singlet that clung to his muscles, and a pair of light blue ripped jeans that were probably against decency laws in some states. I felt heat spread through my body and I had to remind myself to breathe. Then, he leaned in, planting a wet kiss on each cheek. I felt the caress of his hot cheeks on mine.

Dancer: "I'm Joe."

Me: "Hello Joe. I'm Kim."

Joe: "You're hot."

Me: "You're hotter."

The world's shortest conversation was every bit innocent yet flirty. He closed in for a long wet kiss. I had to pull away before the blood rush got to my head. We swapped numbers and I skipped back to the gang.

Everyone was practically begging me for the juicy details, their eyes wide and eager. Tim laughed and applauded me for a job well done. "Kimmie. All my years coming to The Web, I have never been hit on by any man, let alone a hot dancer. You go girl!" The gang dissolved into laughter. Being single was beginning to be fun.

16

Standing On My Own Feet

"All's well that ends well," quipped Shakespeare, but when it came to real life, let's just say it wasn't as easy as writing a play. Jai and I, we hit a few bumps and a few mountains that didn't put us off our quest for our own separate slices of happily ever after.

My transition from four legs good two legs bad, to two legs good four legs bad (a phrase from *Animal Farm*, if you missed the reference) presented almost insurmountable challenges. Firstly, my visa was hanging by a thread. When Jai informed his company of our split, I was given a 'grace period' of two months before my L-1A visa would be revoked. Then, there was the issue of my monthly peanut-sized allowance, which I received as a consultancy fee from my ex-company. It was bundled in Jai's relocation package, which meant that I was about to lose it. Thirdly, the roof over my head had an expiration date. Jai gave me a one-month grace period to stay on.

Well, Tim offered me his pad, but SoHo was where I felt I was destined to be at. Tim's sagely advice contained hard-hitting grains of truth, "SoHo comes at a price, darling." To sum up my misery, I was broke, homeless and on the verge of being deported.

By then, I had taken big juicy chomps out of the Big Apple that I didn't want to stop. I hungered for more. New friends, a lifestyle that was so fabulous, and a future in the Big Apple that was to be rosy-red. Chapter two was supposed to be bigger, better, and bolder. Like everyone else lured by the city's pied piper tunes of better prospects, I fought tooth and nail to stay.

So there I was, strapped into the front seat of an emotional roller coaster, right next to Jai. The ride was a wild one, plunging us into the depths of deep and dark depression. The 'Healing' sign was flashing in the distance, but we couldn't get off the ride, we were stuck in the same rickety cart - living together.

Mentally, we were at different places. While I had already packed up my emotional baggage and checked out, Jai was feeling abandoned and hurt. That made the equation unequal and was the source of our constant friction. I still cared for him but cautiously toed the line to quash his hope of reigniting our extinguished love. Teething phase, to say the least.

Civility largely existed between the two of us. But, with him constantly caught up in his own raging sturm and drang, I never knew what was coming. Dodging Jai became my new cardio workout. Occasionally, I bore the short ends of his sticks, but I kept ploughing on, believing the huge pot of gold at the end of the rainbow was near in sight.

We all get addicted to something that takes the pain away. In Jai's case, if he couldn't be happy, at least he could be drunk. Most days, he'd come home in the wee hours of the morning, legless. I'd hear him bumping into things while I was trying to catch some z's in my luxurious suite above the door. And by suite, I mean a tiny, windowless, dark hole that had a mini staircase leading down to the ground floor. Not exactly the Ritz, but my sights were set on a new life and so this too shall pass.

The loft was an open space with no rooms, no doors, so the acoustics were highly unforgiving. Every little sound echoed like a rock concert in an empty stadium. Things with Jai hit a rock-bottom, I mean he was making noises. Now don't get me wrong, he started bringing ladies back to the house for a little hanky-panky, and I'm as liberal as they come. But seriously, the sounds were so loud and magnified, I wanted to retch, and my sleep was robbed.

That was not all that I was robbed of. The real game-changer was a full-blown robbery. The ladies he'd bring home, they'd snatch up my beauty products and perfume bottles. I started to have a sneaking suspicion that these weren't just your typical one-night standers, but more like ladies of the night.

There I was, coming back from a wild night out with the gang, when I stumbled upon Jai and this unattractive, middle-aged and overweight woman at our door. Jai was clearly three sheets to the wind, wrestling with the keys like they were a Rubik's cube. I decided to be the hero of the hour and take over the door duties. Hysteria took over the lady of the night. She thought I was trying to steal her job. I managed to chase her away. But not without a fracas. Jai and I were so knackered that we crashed fast.

Drastic situations call for drastic measures. When Jai and I woke up, I decided it was time for a serious talk. I told him he could do better than these random women he was splashing his cash for. And also, the thefts. I couldn't resist a jab - I pointed out that his choice of bed warmer the night before was appalling to the core. She was probably the same age as my mom then. We laughed as he blushed.

Come evening, Jai apologized. To sort himself out, he decided he was going to island-hop solo for a month in Thailand. His decision made me happier than a pig in mud. I was thrilled to bits for him to finally get some healing done, all while sipping on cocktails with those cute little umbrellas. And dipping his toes in some fancy pool.

On an equally happy note, I had the loft all to myself. I knew this was God's way to help me get my act together. There was plenty heaped onto my plate. The saying "All's well that ends well" translated to me needing to snag a job, secure a visa, and find my own hip SoHo Pad - all within a month. None of this was an easy feat, now that I was standing on my own two, wobbly feet.

17

The Interviews

Oh, the American Dream. Then, there's the New York dream. Anyone can be a New Yorker. But not everyone gets to stay in New York. Cue in Frank Sinatra's *New York, New York.* Take a minute to google the lyrics. A catchy ditty I'd sing before I packed up and moved to the Big Apple. Next thing I know, it's my personal anthem. I mean, who knew Sinatra was so on point? Anyone who's ever lived in this concrete jungle will tell you, those lyrics hit closer to home.

Competition is rife out there. There's no resting on your laurels. You either swim, sink or live the dream. Everyone's replaceable. Everyone's disposable. You got to be tough. You got to have the chops. You got to play smart. You got to stand out. Sometimes, you got to play dirty.

When it comes to creatives, you're a dime in the dozen. You and every artist, dancer, writer, actor, performer, singer, producer, and director have been seduced by New York's siren song of success. If you can make it big here, you can make it anywhere.

To get my creative foot in the door of Big Apple's advertising world, I had to be, creative. Drop the old "drop-your-book-off-and-hope-for-the-best" routine. I needed to make Creative Directors spit out their fancy, overpriced lattes in pure shock and awe when they saw my book.

My instincts proved right. After I finally scored a role at a top-notch agency, I discovered the competition wasn't just tough, it was like swimming with piranhas. Before we had the luxury of digital portfolios, people would send in actual, physical portfolios from every nook and cranny of America and even around the globe. We're talking thousands of these beefy books, jostling for the limited openings daily.

I was down to a measly sum in my bank. Short on cash but not short on ideas, I came up with this genius plan: a direct mail pack. Inside was a pair of the thickest, woolliest socks. Alongside the socks was my book, also known as my portfolio of past work. And just to make sure they got the joke, I included a card that read "I'm about to knock your socks off". And then they'd need the new socks.

There was no bank breaking as I got the socks and boxes on the cheap from Century 21. The socks were warm gestures to keep their feet toasty, in the dead of winter.

I dug up the names of the big shot Executive Creative Directors and Creative Directors at the top 20 agencies I was eyeing. Did I have a tough decision to make. It was a toss-up between indulging in my favorite smoked salmon and cream cheese bagels for the upcoming week, or keeping someone's feet warm in the hopes of landing a job.

Let me tell you about the serendipitous way I stumbled into the world of advertising in Singapore. Advertising wasn't even on my radar. As fate would have it, the universe had a funny plan up its sleeve. I came across an ad for a Senior Copywriter role at a world-renowned, legendary and award-winning agency in Singapore. Brazenly, I applied for the position I had no business applying for. Not a smidgen of copywriting experience to my name. If fortune favors the bold, I lucked out big time. I was asked to interview.

I was 15 minutes away from my face-to-face interview when I decided to phone a friend - a former strategist at an agency. If I'm going into battle, I might as well have a game plan. Even she knew that 15 minutes was hardly enough time to perform miracles. So, she gave me a golden nugget. She told me, "There are two categories of advertising work. One is above-the-line and the other is below-the-line. You're better off requesting below-the-line work to start off with. "

I thanked her for her time, still confused as a chameleon in a bag of Skittles. Apparently, in ad-speak, "above-the-line" is all about the glitzy, glamorous stuff like TV and print ads. You know, the kind of work that makes you feel like Don Draper, strutting around in a sharp suit, sipping an old-fashioned. On the other hand, "below-the-line" is the advertising equivalent of doing your own laundry - necessary, but not exactly thrilling. It's the digital, direct mail, and retail stuff that doesn't exactly scream 'Mad Men'. My ex-colleague was basically saying that it's easier to sneak into the advertising party through the back door by being willing to handle the less-glamorous tasks.

I completely botched the interview. The Creative Director asked me for my "book". I looked at him like he just asked me for the moon. I didn't have one. Now, you'd think I couldn't make things worse. I went ahead and pulled out a truly horrendous Sony Ericsson phone ad that nobody, and I mean nobody, had asked for. The Director had his face in his hands, probably wondering how he ended up wasting an hour of his precious life with me. At this point, I figured it was the perfect time to play my below-the-line card.

Me: "I am sorry if I had wasted your time. If it's possible, I'd like to start with below-the-belt work.

Creative Director: "What?"

Me: "I'd like to start with below-the-belt work."

The Creative Director, an ancient and rotund fellow donned in a billowing tunic, started a cackling fit so mighty, I feared he might keel over and die from a heart attack. I accidentally suggested "below-the-belt work" when what I actually meant was "below-the-line work". No one had to loosen their belts or anything scandalous like that. God forbid. I was good entertainment, and he thought I was mad to turn up for the interview.

As a reward for my tenacity, he gave me a creative test assignment. I had to deconstruct a bad print ad and turn in an alternative. I eagerly took up the gauntlet, directed my footsteps to the bookstore and shelled out my hard-earned cash on the priciest advertising magazine they had. I picked up the ropes, pronto, on how to create ads and handed in my work. Then, a few days later, the phone rang.

Creative Director: "I've got news for you. Do you want to hear the good or the bad?"

Me: "The bad."

Creative Director: "The bad news is that you didn't get the Senior Copywriter position."

Me: "What's the good news then?"

Creative Director: "I'm creating a Copywriter position especially for you."

Just like that, I got my entrance ticket to advertising. But if you're thinking it was all candy floss and lollipop trees, let me burst that bubble for you. It was pure hell working for him, a trio of sexist, misogynist and bully. I wasn't the only one on his hit parade. I remember, me and another female Copywriter, were roped in for weekend pitches, which involved taking minutes at pitch meetings and playing barista to senior male staff. We thought we'd been called up to the major leagues, but we became service staff by sheer virtue of our gender.

My mom was in the hospital getting her toe amputated because of a gnarly diabetic infection. My request for a day off was flatly declined, without rhyme or reason, by the mean Creative Director. I packed up my work, took it to the hospital, and spread it out on the floor. This while my mom had her toe hacked off. That piece of work went on to win first prize at a prestigious award show.

On a thankful note, he kick-started my thrilling roller coaster ride into the exhilarating world of advertising. I learned so many writing tricks from him that I started racking up industry vanity awards. Unsure if karma had a hand, he died a few years after. He was diagnosed with liver cancer and his dying wish was to become a Creative Director. Just like he once handed me my golden ticket to adland, someone did the same for him. He had been dealt the death card when he interviewed me.

Back to the socks. Two months in and I had managed to knock a few pairs off. A year after 9/11, the economy was still reeling in from the aftermath. Recovery was slow and the government upped the criteria for non-Americans to get jobs in the US. Understandably, priority went to Americans. Companies had to produce reams of documentation that they couldn't find the right American for the job and that hiring a foreign talent was the last resort.

Scoring an interview was tough. When I landed one, I'd treat it like a royal event. On one such occasion, I decided to go for an androgynous look – a snazzy beige suede jacket worn over a crisp white long-sleeve shirt, paired with matching beige trousers. The look was complete with a silver tie borrowed from Jai. I had my New York State Identification Card photo shoot right after the interview. Talk hitting two birds with one well-dressed stone.

The interview went south. The Creative Director and

I had about as much chemistry as oil and water. Feeling like I'd just flushed a golden opportunity down the toilet, I was in a foul mood. With a mood darker than Darth Vader's wardrobe, I trudged to the New York State Identification Cards processing center. After the paperwork, I ambled over to the photo counter to get my mug shot snapped for my new ID. A staff member, who seemed as interested in his job as a cat is in a bath, ushered me towards a stool. He tinkered with it until I matched its height or it matched mine. Then he disappeared behind the camera.

I forced on a smile. After holding my smile for what felt like an eternity, my patience evaporated, and I let my smile drop and furrowed my brows. And then...FLASH! Before I knew it, my scowling, about-to-throw-a-tantrum face was immortalized on my New York ID. The photographer refused to take another shot.

Interview dramas were plenty. Like this one mishap at a café prior to an interview. Seriously, I could win an award for being Almost Late. So, I hatched a master plan - to get to the café, conveniently located under the building of my soon-to-be disaster of an interview, an hour early. Then, with 15 minutes left, I gulped down the leftover coffee, grabbed my portfolio bag, and sprinted towards the counter to pay.

I was just about to give myself a medal for being Ms. Punctuality when suddenly, smoke started billowing from behind the counter. I peered over and saw orange flames licking at the heel of the counter staff, whose face was drained of color. A white plume of smoke took over the small café. She grabbed a fire extinguisher and aimed it at the flames dancing in a bin. White foam blanketed the fire and it fizzled to its death. I checked my watch and knew I had five minutes for a high-speed vertical marathon up the building.

I sauntered into the reception a casual five minutes past the deadline, panting like a dog on a hot summer's day. The receptionist gave me a look and pointed me towards the office of the Executive Creative Director. Once I entered, he scanned me wordlessly up and down. Stunned, he pointed at my face and started doing this weird air-circling thing with his finger. He managed to find his words and said, "You've got foam all over your face... your neck... and your shirt." I raised my shaky hands to my face and sure enough, I felt the foam on my cheeks, forehead, chin and neck.

I did a turn and caught my reflection in the window. I looked like a confused marshmallow man, my face all frosted up apart from two peephole eyes. Then, the penny dropped. The fire extinguisher had gone all party popper on me.

In my befuddled state, I politely asked for a break to visit the ladies room. I could feel the all-seeing eyes of the Executive Creative Director boring into my back like laser beams as I sashayed my way to the ladies room, head held high. Once the door mercifully clicked shut behind me, I went after the paper towels like a mad man grasping at straws. I scrubbed my face free of the thick foam and watched my complexion shift from a ghostly Casper white to a tomato red.

I waltzed back into the Executive Creative Director's office with all the faux dignity I could muster, trying to brush off the comedy of errors that had just unfolded. Soon, there was another dumpster fire waiting for me. This time, it was my temper. He casually mentioned he just wanted a friendly meet with a Singaporean creative after hearing about our epic trophy haul. There was no Copywriter position. The Casper episode haunted me for a long time.

"Kimmie, you've got enough material for a best-seller on botched interviews!" Tim chuckled, nursing his vanilla Stolichnaya vodka and tonic over rocks. I dramatically flung my hands in the air, playing along with his jest. Fast forward two months and I landed a Creative Copywriter gig at one of New York's top advertising agencies.

18

Love Loft to Party Loft

When you're scraping the bottom of the barrel, the only way out is up. Things started looking up for me, maybe because I showed mettle in battling the almost impossible odds of staying on.

The joyous journey of visa paperwork started after I put pen to paper on that contract. I had to get all sorts of testimonials from past employers. The ad agency hired a third-party credential evaluation company to scrutinize my academic and past work credentials. The process took six months. Post 9/11, they really amped up on the red tape.

Meanwhile, I stumbled upon a tiny co-op apartment at 349 West Broadway between Broome and Grand Street, three streets away from our Varick loft. Talk about divine intervention. I got to stay in my beloved SoHo neighborhood. Co-ops are usually in historic buildings, and this one was no exception. For a mere $1500 a month, which to New Yorkers is akin to finding a Picasso at a yard sale, I had landed a gem.

It was as if the Universe had finally tired of my relentless optimism and decided to line up my ducks in a row, probably just to shut me up. It was all nothing short of a miracle.

So, there I was, squeezed between the joy of freedom and the excitement of new beginnings. I had to vacate the Varick loft when Jai came back from his *Eat, Pray, Love* in Thailand. He had graciously agreed to an extended stay as the loft was vacant anyway. The keys to my very own loft were going to be mine in two weeks, and the countdown to the moveout began. Post break-up, and with Jai gone, the love loft morphed into a party loft.

When the cat was away, me and the merry gang transformed the Varick loft into the hottest party spot in town every Friday and Saturday. But once Monday rolled around, that party palace turned into my personal pressure cooker. I was juggling the job hunt, counting pennies, and sweating about my visa situation. Parties didn't cost me an arm or a leg. Everyone brought drinks and nibbles. Interestingly, the parties turned into a real-life game of six degrees of separation. Everyone invited their mates, who then blabbed to their mates, and before you knew it, we had a party chain reaction on our hands.

When Jai was around, parties wrapped up early as he

wearied easily. But us? We had more in the tank and chased more revelry at bars in SoHo or Chelsea after our parties. With Jai gone, parties ended at whatever o'clock. Usually, I only realized it was over when I got a rude awakening, often in the form of a cushion imprint on my face. Looking around, it was a battlefield of after-party casualties. People sprawled across the day bed, slumped on cushions, still dressed to impress in their party clothes.

Tim took himself off the market after he found a partner, Simon, after a long single spell. When we were both single, we had more dating disasters than *Will and Grace* and *Sex and the City* racked up. But unlike those TV shows, our dating lives didn't come with a script. We genuinely thought we were doomed to a lifetime of singlehood.

In half jest and in half seriousness, Tim joked about his retirement plan: buying a house in the boondocks of Tennessee. In his last days, he'd get a shot gun and a pit bull. With his last breath, he'd shoot himself with the shotgun and have the pit bull devour him. Now, he might have to eat his own words. Tim has been playing house with Simon for over two decades. So, it's *Aged and the City* for them.

The three of us crafted a rollicking roller coaster of rib-tickling, gut-busting hilarity. Remember our reunion dinner at OXO Tower Restaurant, Bar and Brasserie in London? Simon reminded me of our Christmas party story that was conveniently buried in the sands of time. He dusted the side-splitting story off and recounted it to my thirteen-year-old son, Noah and two of my friends. When I remembered the incident, I couldn't resist adding my own brand of glitter and tinsel to Simon's version. Here's the story, sans our animated body language.

We hosted a Christmas party at the Varick loft while Jai drunk-sipped his cocktails somewhere in Thailand. In terms of accolades, it was the biggest, the most fun, and the penultimate hurrah before I packed up my belongings and bid adieu to the loft. We were all wasted close to midnight but let's be honest, that was pretty much par for the course for us. At 11.59 P.M., Simon reached into his shirt pocket and pulled out a handful of cigars, passing them out like candy at a parade. We were all lit up for a proper Christmas smoke out, but not a single one of us had a lighter. Then, like a light bulb going off, I had a brilliant idea – I could use my trusty, old-school gas stove to light up our stogies.

I drunk-tottered to the ancient gas stove and struggled-ignited it a few times until a chorus line of tiny blue flames started their performance. My eyelids were shutting on me as I had had one over the eight. Shoving the cigar between my lips, I leaned in for a fiery kiss. For a few seconds, I surrendered to my heavy eyelids, and soon a burnt smell wafted up my nose like incense. Eyes popping open like surprised jack-in-the-boxes, I spotted the singed bits of my fringe falling. Disoriented, I spun around to face the gang.

"Oh my God Kimmie!" Tim squeaked. "Your bangs are burned!" Sud exclaimed, nearly choking on his wine. This sudden burst of hilarity was unexpected in the typically mellow ambiance of the OXO Tower Restaurant, Bar and Brasserie in London, 20 years on.

For months, I worked on growing out my damn bangs. Instead of my normal sleek fringe, I was sporting these weird and awkward short stumps which looked like stumped pubes. The inquisitive glances and outright questions from friends and random passersby were relentless. I found myself retelling the same absurd tale over and over. It became a repetitive note to self to never, ever try to light a cigar over a kitchen stove.

At the same party where my bangs singed to stumped pubes, Simon got as drunk as a skunk and did the biggest spew into Jai's beloved cavernous decorative clay pot. Normally, Tim and Simon would be the clean-up crew. But this time, we left Simon's spew in the pot and prayed that we'd get away with murder, which we did.

My last month in the loft was a hoot with some oddball happenings. Our neighbor, a fashion photographer named Phil, was in his late 50s, lanky with dirty blonde hair. Nothing about his looks was striking, but his wardrobe was an entirely different story. He usually leveled up his simple silhouette with brow-raising lime green, tangerine, sunflower yellow or Nantucket red form-fitting chino trousers, anchored with plain white tee and a colorful scarf tied around his pencil-thin neck. As far as etiquette went, we'd politely greet each other whenever we bumped into him in the apartment or at our local hangout, Café Noir.

One fateful evening, while I was painting the town red with the gang at Café Noir, I chanced upon Phil. He caught on quick that I'd been flying solo quite a bit and asked after Jai. I told him we broke up and Jai was somewhere in Thailand, getting his feet all powdered by that sugar-sand beach. Phil asked if I was game for a few test shots. Now that piqued my interest and flattered my ego. He promptly extended an invite to his pad for the very next day.

The following afternoon, I made a grand entrance into his loft, which was also his photo studio. My eyes widened, this place was bigger, brighter and more spacious than our loft. It felt less a home and more like a photography battlefield with lighting, screens and camera stands marching around like soldiers. Professional cameras were positioned strategically like generals overseeing the operations.

The place was a fashion magazine jungle, with flashy, colorful, black and white magazines stacked in piles against the walls, forming a glossy paper fort. His coffee table had been conquered by photography books and fashion magazines. And there was this screen stand, standing all high and mighty at the corner, that partitioned his sleeping quarters from his workspace.

He greeted me with enthusiasm, planting a smooch on each of my cheeks before gesturing grandly to the couch. He who wields the power steers the conversation. Small talk was initiated to break the ice, before diving headfirst into the deep ocean of his photography experiences. Clearly a novice, I just nodded along, trying not to look too clueless. I'd been part of some advertising shoots, but fashion photography was alien to me.

Then he leaned in for the kill. He picked up a photography book with a gorgeous black and white image of a woman's bare back on the front cover. He casually flipped through the pages, revealing a few discerning spreads that perfectly combined subtle female nudity with style. "I whipped up this little number a few years back. The publisher's practically begging me for a sequel." He turned to the back of the book, flashing the prominent publisher's logo. Impressed, I replied, "Stunning pictures."

He tossed the book onto the cluttered coffee table, sat back and stretched his arms along the length of the sofa. It felt like an amped-up power move. "I'd like to feature you in it. We can start with some test shots if you're up for it."

Used to the unusual in New York, this was another add to the colorful collection. But something didn't feel right to me, and you always go with your gut. "That's lovely of you to ask. I'll think about it."

I managed to extricate myself from his web of power games, and never got in touch. I kept up my etiquette, whenever I saw him at Café Noir, even after I moved to my swanky new loft. I still can't figure out if his invitation was genuine. It smacked of an exceedingly common photographer's repertoire that ensnared many unsuspecting girls. It was down to the fall of the dice, and I chose not to play that game.

Remember hot dancer Joe? We finally went out on a

date, and it was a revelation. Turns out, "Joe" was just his stage name. His real name was something far more exotic, a Romanian name that rolled off the tongue like a rich red wine. But he didn't live by the rules of authenticity and that didn't sit well with me. Back in Romania, he was a professional wrestler. But like every other small-town boy with a big dream, he set off for the bright lights of the Big Apple, hoping to make it big. He ended up dancing around poles in gay clubs and performing the occasional striptease at private parties.

We had a bit of fun at the loft, which goes down as one of the best loft memories. The man was an irresistible sex symbol. My last good memory of Joe is him rolling off the bed, wrestling to get his tight jeans over those beefy, sculpted legs of his. Classic blue jeans paired with a jacked-up upper torso is a timeless sexy combination you don't ever tire of.

"I've enjoyed that. I've never had an Asian girl. Would you be my Asian girl?" Joe blurted out, as if I was some exotic dish on the oriental menu that he had sampled and wished to order again. I searched for words, but none came. "I want you to be my Asian girl", he concluded. We kissed and he left. I was left with a strange aftertaste. I didn't want to see him after that.

Tim, Sud and Vinny grilled me for every juicy detail in a no-holds-barred, tell-all session. Tim was trying his best to contain his excitement, for fear of getting an earful from Simon. The gang was in stitches, howling with laughter at every 'intimate' description of Joe's physique, performance, and his 'stamina'.

I had a short dalliance with my neighbor, Anton, during that cold winter month of bed-warming fun. After one of our wild loft parties, we all crammed into the lift. And there he was, Anton, standing in the corner with a crooked grin. Even though we shared a roof, we'd never actually met. But that night, amidst the giggles and hiccups, we finally exchanged hellos. He passed me his business card.

A Jewish American teetering on the edge of 50 with a mop of salt and pepper curls. Anton stood at a mere 5 feet 7. While his height held little allure for me, he exuded a certain magnetism. He was a stickler for appearances – his skin was always perfectly tanned (thanks to the trusty sun bed), and his physique well-honed at the gym. A business owner and true-blue bachelor, he put in long hours at work. His bachelordom was reflected in his loft which was larger than ours and boasted an enviable pool table and a bar.

Gentlemanly, spontaneous and congenial, Anton

made an excellent bedfellow and companion, capable of scintillating conversations. He even popped up at a few of our loft parties, and the gang just ate him up.

However, our age gap was a crevasse which yawned at our feet. After we rang in the New Year with one hell of a party, it was goodbye Anton and Varick loft.

19

349 West Broadway

Nestled in the bustling street of West Broadway, between Broome and Grand Street, sits the charming 349 West Broadway apartment. This historic gem dates back to 1900 and it's fronted by a teeny-weeny, blink and you'll miss it green door.

While it's within a short walking distance from the old Varick loft, it felt like I'd traveled afar to get to my new SoHo pad. After hurdling over job applications, visa paperwork, and the dreaded apartment search, a lot more legwork was required. Next challenge: the staircase. Now, this wasn't just any staircase. This was a steep, winding, and downright dizzying path to my new loft, at the top of this seven-story walk-up. Now, I know what you're thinking, seven stories is a piece of cake. It felt like I had conquered seventy flights of stairs when I got to the top.

Guests arrived huffing and puffing, one hand clinging to the wall for dear life, the other dramatically draped over their hip. Their chests heaved like they'd just run a marathon, and their faces were so red. No words were needed. I'd get them water, drinks, or anything to appease them. And in the summer, it wasn't just collapsed lungs they had to contend with. With the heat, they were entirely drenched in sweat.

"What a climb, Kimmie," they'd huff and puff, everyone from Tim to Jai, saving their last breath for a final lament. We never got used to it. Like brave warriors, Tim, Simon and Claire helped me with my move. After it was all done, they collapsed on the floor like wounded warriors. Not a twitch from any of them. I did what any self-respecting, newly moved-in person would do - ordered pizza. With a heroic dash of my own, I jogged down and up the dreaded stairs one last time. All for the common good.

It wasn't just any old key my landlord slipped into my hands. Nope, it was a VIP, exclusive pass to the rooftop. Who knew I was getting my own personal party penthouse in the sky? That rooftop became the stage for countless epic parties. Under a blanket of stars, I added twinkling fairy lights, a jumble of chairs and tables, and the ambiance was cranked up a few notches.

There are 24 little units in the co-op apartment. Most stuff is a google search away and I was overcome by acute nostalgia when I stumbled upon my old unit listed on a property site. Sold for $575,000 on March 3rd, 2022, it now has a new owner.

The small studio with the little alcove has had a bit of a glow-up. There's brand-new kitchen cabinetry, modern fittings in the long bathroom with walk-in wardrobe flanking both sides, and new stairs that lead up to the alcove. Disappointingly, they've covered up the skylight in the alcove, knocking points off charm. I used to lie on my bed, gazing up at the sky through that skylight, watching the snow and rain fall like a scene from a romantic movie.

At our recent reunion dinner at OXO Restaurant in London, Tim and Simon were rolling around in laughter, recalling those wild parties we used to throw. I reminded Tim about that time he decided to christen my brand new sink with his dinner.

Another reason for a party came in the form of housewarming and the usual suspects were invited. Tim was so boozed up and ended up chundering into the sink. Thought he was being sneaky, but come morning, his regurgitated party snacks were popping up like a homemade science volcano. I hit the roof and raged at Tim about some mystery moron's gastric assault on my pristine sink. Grinning like a

Cheshire cat, he admitted it was him. You just can't stay mad at a guy who confesses with a grin like that.

At the restaurant, we were all belly-laughing over the 'weeded-out hysterical cat story'. Not a single party would pass without Tim and Simon smoking weed. So, at this one particular bash, a guest brought a cat she was babysitting. Poor little thing was scared out of its whiskers by the constant human parade and the cacophony of voices in the apartment, so it decided to hide in one of the two walk-in closets bordering the long bathroom. Sticking to their usual routine, Tim and Simon locked themselves inside the bathroom to savor their top-shelf spliff. Before you knew it, a queue for the bathroom started forming, so I did a courtesy knock on the door.

Simon swung open the door. Out of nowhere, the cat catapulted towards me, like a Jack-in-the-box gone rogue. First it screeched and flashed its teeth, swayed side-to-side like a drunken sailor and finally conked out. We all watched this feline melodrama unfold and concluded - the weed smoke must've given it a solid high. Everyone at the party and OXO restaurant erupted into fits of laughter.

The loft became the people's loft, with anywhere from fifty to seventy folks milling about. And it wasn't just our usual crew - Kaylee, Jai, the office gang, and friends of friends of friends of... well, you get the idea. We had random people off the street joining in the fun too. With the constant parade of people marching up and down the building, some passersby and tourists got the wrong idea. They thought my rooftop was a happening bar.

We didn't turn them away. The only membership fee to join our merry band was to pop round to the booze shop and grab a couple of bottles. You wouldn't believe the wild mix we had. People from every corner of the globe, every walk of life - it was like the United Nations, but with more tequila.

There were times when I hit the sauce so hard, I was out cold before the clock struck twelve. How I ever navigated those Mount Everest-like stairs to my little alcove of a bed while hammered is a mystery. As the saying 'mi casa su es casa' goes, the gang shouldered on with the host duties. It was a regular occurrence for friends to show up after I had already checked out for the evening. They'd ask for me, and Tim and Simon would direct their gaze to my lifeless body sprawled out on my bed and say, "Oh, she passed out two hours ago."

Friday, Saturday, Sunday - you name it, we partied. Mi casa, mi rules. The clean-up crew – Tim and Simon, along with Sud, Claire, Sid and Vinny, swooped in to whisk away countless clanging bottles to the trash. We kept the neighbors' complaints at bay by adding them to the VIP section of our invite list.

Kaylee was always kicking back at the loft. Her car, which proudly sported Jersey plates, seemed to have taken root down by the apartment. She turned parking lot hunting into *Hunger Games* sport, as parking spots didn't come easy on my street.

After I'd flown the coop, Jai and I rekindled our friendship. We were living it up, hitting our favorite hangouts - the bars, the eateries, the cafes. He dropped by to chill at my loft and most importantly, he was my toilet paper fairy godmother. You see, I have this strange aversion to carrying toilet paper from the store. Jai, knowing my peculiar phobia, would come around and stock up my toilet paper supply before he'd jet off on his long business trips.

For a few wild years, 349 West Broadway was the address of fun for all of us. If walls could talk, those ones would probably recount tales of love, heartbreaks, and a rollercoaster of hope and despair. Not to forget, endless entertaining conversations overheard at parties.

20

Roller Skate Rink Kink

Ask any fabulous gay about the crème de la crème of New York City's dance party scene, and *Roxy Saturdays* would undoubtedly rank high on his list. One of the biggest gay dance nights where you dance your night away in your glitter wear, the NYC staple featured a stellar line-up of top-notch live DJs like Paul van Dyk, David Guetta, Victor Calderone, and Junior Vasquez.

Roxy took up a sprawling space at 17th Street in Chelsea, the gay epicenter of NYC. Dubbed 'Studio 54 of the roller rinks', it had its rolling heydays in the 1980s as a roller skate rink. More than that, it became an emblematic New York hot spot which opened its doors to multi-ethnic and gender bender clubbers, way ahead of the LGBT woke culture of the early 2010s.

Typical *Roxy Saturdays* were over the top, wild, raucous, daring and outrageous. Sometimes, you'd be rubbing shoulders, amongst other forms of rubs, with the legendary who's who of NYC's colorful scene. Most clubbers pranced around in outlandish and creative outfits, offering a sensational visual display. The vibes were unmatched. No wonder our gang made it our official Saturday hangout.

The lure of unlimited alcohol deals had us charging in bright-eyed-bushy-tailed and stumbling out staggeringly wasted. For the gay boys in the gang, this was their ultimate gay mingle and high-octane all-nighter. Lesbian Claire and straight me were more than happy to play supporting roles in this fabulous drama. After all, the stage belonged to the gays.

One evening we were there, the house music boomed, the atmosphere was top-tier, and I dare add - more intimate than usual. An uncommonly long conga line of gay men had formed on the dance floor, which greatly piqued my interest. And once I gave the gang the heads up, their eyebrows were sky-high too. This wasn't the line for the free-flow drinks, so the gang decided to get to the bottom of things, by getting to the front of the line.

With barely any wiggle room, we bravely formed a line and slithered our way through the crowd. Some in the line were lost in the pulsating music, while others were having a good chat with fellow queuers. By then, our curiosity peaked. We closed in on a rickety, metal staircase, which led to a narrow ledge where a smattering of clubbers occasionally engaged in a spot of people watching. From up there, you get a bird's eye view of the club, and let me tell you, the people-watching was primo. The line of men extended all the way to the far-right corner of the ledge.

What we saw next was debauchery on another level. Picture this, around 15 guys, perched on a ledge, pants down around their ankles, and hips gyrating. The lone ranger at the far end of this human line was having his whistle blown by the first man standing in line. The first man in line was penetrated by the one behind him. The whole scene was a daisy chain of unadulterated debauchery, each pushing the pace. In pure mechanical clockwork, the seated man zipped up his pants, zipped down the stairs, leaving his throne ready for the next in line.

I could safely say it was the most peculiar gay orgy we'd ever witnessed. A definite first and last for me, I wished I could unsee what I saw. Glued to the floor in pure shock, we watched the scene unfold like a well-choreographed yet somewhat risqué ballet. It was a mashup of elegance and effrontery, like watching swans waltzing in a mud bath. Distasteful? Sure.

Sud's got his comedic timing down pat. He quipped,

"At least this line moves fast. We should have had the heads-up at the end of the line that those at the front were giving heads." We all burst into giggles, deciding to retreat to the bar for some good, clean fun. The wild party happening nearby was a tad too spicy for our vanilla tastes.

'Another one bites the dust' may be common in the fickle club scene but Roxy kept the roller wheels going for 25 years. The mirror ball was finally taken down in 2007. Notoriously difficult to get into but not notorious for sordid acts, I wonder if the management knew about the orgy.

21

Diamonds Became This Girl's Best Friend

The city that never sleeps is also the city that never ceases to surprise you. A shining example of a surprise was my diamond runner gig in the Diamond District at 47th Street between Fifth and Sixth Avenues. Not one to take a shine to diamonds, this came completely out of left field.

Tim had a vast rolodex of Malaysian gay contacts. And among the motley crew, there was this one character, Calvin, who was a real piece of work. Tim was sometimes a magnet attracting troubled souls, given his bubbly nature, high tolerance for pain and pain-in-the-butt friends. Calvin was a drama queen, neither a 'peachy bitchy' nor a 'bitchy bitchy' but had his own category - 'bitchy bitchy bitchy'. Wary of him, I always kept him at an arm's length. He had little to offer and I knew little about him.

Enter Ronan, Calvin's Irish boyfriend who was formerly a priest turned jewelry designer. Talk about a career change. Now try to picture this, twenty years back, a gay priest. An Irish gay priest at that. His home turf must have been abuzz with gossip. His sexuality must have challenged his religion from within, which could have lent him the impetus to hop on a plane to the Big Apple, where he would be accepted.

Calvin's relationship with his beau was like a rollercoaster ride that gave your life's energy a black hole-level suction. It was so intense that my ears learned to play deaf early on. Here's the short of the long why Calvin clung onto the relationship, according to close sources.

Ronan was loaded. How an Irish priest ended up with more dough than a bakery, I'll never know. Calvin was holed up in Ronan's colossal Connecticut mansion, living the high life and not paying a dime. The plot thickened as he schemed to have Ronan to invest in his "business plans".

Out of nowhere, Ronan needed a helping hand for a jewelry trade show in Orlando. Free as a bird as I was waiting for my visa approval, Calvin thought I'd be the right person. The gig was a boon for my dire financial situation, as they were offering a small stipend. And get this, Calvin, the King of Cheap, even promised to cover my modest meals. And to top it all off, I got a free flight to Orlando.

Well, on the downside, I found myself rooming with

Ronan - a complete stranger. What about my personal space, you might ask. I knew nothing about the jewelry world too. And let's not forget my stint as a Sub-Editor for two trade journals that were about as exciting as watching paint dry. Yes, I knew trade shows, but sales?

Have you ever met someone who exuded such bad vibes that all your internal alarm bells didn't just ring, but your system short circuits too? That was Ronan for me. Met him an hour before our flight and let me tell you, I had to leverage on all my reserves of sanity, civility and politeness in exchange for fragile peace.

Power and ego changed all dynamics. When we arrived at the trade show, it was like Ronan morphed into some kind of diva. Suddenly, his definition of "assistance" included ironing his clothes and cleaning his shoes. Our expectations were totally misaligned. I thought I signed up to help with business stuff, not become his personal butler.

There I was, putting my foot down, refusing to be treated like a second-class citizen when his demands turned into a circus act. From being a high-nosed snob with his veiled threats, he morphed into a monstrous, rude, nasty, temperamental diva. And you thought the drama ends after work hours. We were cooped up in a hotel room that was tiny, so there was no respite from him, and his black cloud of negativity was exploding my head.

Thank heavens that by day two, I was already making friends. Jolly Jewish diamond jewelers who took up stands across us were quick to pick up the hairy dynamics between Ronan and me. Feeling downright sorry for me, they kept my spirits up with endless banter, jokes and invited me for meals at their own expense. I wore gratitude on my sleeve towards them, as they were my much-needed salve.

With a card out of torment, I politely gave the old devil the slip at dinner. I sashayed my way over to this jolly group of diamond jewelers and had a shimmering good time. The second evening wore on and one of them jeweler fellas seemed to sparkle a little more my way.

Saul, a strapping young bachelor in his 30s, was a Jewish American who was born in Israel and then made the trek over to the land of stars and stripes. Meanwhile, the rest of the jewelers, all hitched and comfortably nestled in their 40s and 50s, were starting to feel their age. Past midnight, their batteries wound down and sputtered.

Saul and I trooped on, hitting a litany of bars through Orlando, which was a welcome change from the soul-crushing monotony of the trade exhibition hall and the hotel room that was about as cozy as Alcatraz. Sparks flew between us like a faulty electric socket. We smooched on the second night and by the third, we were going out post-dinner with the band of jewelers.

On the last day of the trade show, I swapped digits with some sparkly diamond dealers. Saul, a non-New Yorker, turned out to be my Autumn romance. We decided to part ways when the leaves fell, but he's still lingering on my Linkedin contacts.

A few weeks down the line, one of the diamond jewelers from the Big Apple asked if I was game for a job working for his friend from Armenia. One for cultural diversity, this was getting interesting as I'd never rubbed elbows with Armenians before. I quickly clarified that I was more of a corporate ilk, just twiddling my thumbs for my visa for my new gig to get the green light.

I also explained the diamond world was one which I was untrained for. But he swiftly dismissed the lack of knowledge and experience with a confident note, "You'll learn. You're a fast learner and a smart cookie." Sold. Just like that, I was thrusted into the bling-bling diamond universe in the Diamond District.

22

All that Glitters is Not Gold. Nor Diamond.

The icy Diamond District lost its luster on me, post my initiation into its chilly folds, during the bitter-cold winter. It's a peculiar place, like a double-sided coin. One side is a shopper's paradise. The other side is a dark underbelly privy to those who work there. The use of present tense stems from my firm belief that it still runs on the same modus operandi.

Nitid side one is what buyers see when they head there to shop for diamonds. Here, we have two types of customers. First, we have the lovebirds on the hunt for the perfect piece of bling to cement their undying love. Engagement rings, wedding rings, necklaces that range from affordable to bank breaking. Young love and disposable income make a great combo. But my absolute favorites? The sweet, innocent, about-to-pop-the-question guys who wouldn't know a carat from a carrot. They're so desperate for a ring they'll fall for every trick in the sales book.

There are those informed and savvy shoppers who are

well-versed in the inner workings of the diamond district. They come strutting in with their designs all figured out, and they head straight for the sparkliest of sparklies. Then, they sweet talk the jewelers into crafting their dream bling.

Oh, side two, the complex underbelly of the Diamond District. A place where Jewish Americans, Israelis, and Russian Jews (who took a slight detour through Israel before arriving in the Big Apple) are all hard at work. And let's not forget about the Armenians who sometimes squared off in a friendly diamond duel with the Jewish community, other times joining forces in the pursuit of that perfect gem.

This world is so complicated that it warrants a book for an entire dissect. In the interest of brevity, I'll sum it up – jewelers are always in competition, but also depend on each other. They're all connected in a deep, often ethnic and nationalistic bling-bling network. It's a very complex and intricate network.

When a customer rocks up and requests a diamond of specific color and grade that the jeweler doesn't have in stock, he calls up his connections, who are also his competitors, in search of this diamond. This wild goose chase can take anywhere from a few nail-biting minutes to days filled with caffeine-fueled suspense. But the mission is clear: find that diamond and get it for a steal, because let's face it, everyone loves a good bargain.

I once asked my boss Tamar, who hailed from the exotic lands of Armenia, why no one ever tried their luck at robbing the diamond district. With a mischievous twinkle in his eye, he revealed that the district was crawling with plainclothes police. You see, those men you thought were having a casual chat over coffee and bagels? Undercover cops. Years ago, a foolhardy robber had a bullet put in his head when he decided to rob a store.

Tamar had this little bitty stand in The Arcade, a fancy-pants jewelry store packed with other jewelers selling shiny diamonds, swanky fine jewelry and precious gemstones. Tamar wasn't one of the high rollers, mind you. But, he did have a steady parade of customers looking for pocket-friendly pieces.

The big fish in the bling-bling pond reel in customers with bigger bank accounts. They count celebrities as their regular customers and accessorize the hip hop world. Hip Hop legend Missy Elliot is a walking dazzling showcase of bold and outsized custom fine jewelry such as braid-thick gold chains, diamond encrusted pendants and other bling that come in all forms. Going big is her game but you wouldn't spot her in the

Diamond District. Instead, she deployed her bling brigade to get her flashy statement pieces custom made. We could spot those guys a mile away - they were an ominous squad draped in gold.

Jackass star Steve-O made a humble appearance at the high roller's booth across from us. Beyond the stunts he pulled, he probably understood aesthetic relevance. I quietly enjoyed the humor of my own journey to this glittering world of the diamond district. Bling it on.

While there were sparkly sides to working in the diamond district, Tamar took out some of the shine. A temperamental, leery tightwad in his 60s, he cut a classic villainous look with dark menacing eyes, silvery curls, crusty skin and a bushy and unkempt unibrow. His short fuse and even shorter stature made him a walking, talking Napoleon complex. Dandruff generously dusted his shoulders. His breath was so rank that flowers would wilt instantaneously if he breathed onto them.

When conversing with me, he leaned in so close that I had to hold my breath until I turned blue or risk wilting like the flowers. His shameless flirtations induced a deep retch of everything I ate for the week. His hand placed on my waist or on my face made me recoil like I had touched acid.

Misery loves company. Meet Anna, my partner in retail crime - a part-time Turkish sales assistant who shared my shift at Tamar's modest stand. We were both worked to the bone and our shared suffering bonded us. A 'peachy bitchy' with a sharp humor, she made Tamar the victim of her endless, hilarious rants.

I was a bit of a diamond runner and salesgirl. I'm not exactly a natural hustler, more like a brutally honest person. What I'm good at, is seeing the good in something, that is, if it exists. In the wild world of advertising and marketing, I'm all about creating a good spin. I can take a credible positioning and whip up a narrative around it.

However, I am unable to position something I do not believe in. Simply put, I am incapable of lying or running contrary to my thoughts. I can't even tell a white lie without staying up all night worrying about it. In my world of sales, it was more like a treasure hunt. Customers were the adventurers, and I was their trusty guide, helping them find that perfect piece of bling. I didn't trick them into buying stuff they don't want or need. No sneaky snake oil tricks.

Tamar, who knew I couldn't sell water to a fish, decided to put me on runner duty instead. Whenever he got those weird custom jewelry requests, I was the one who had to take care of them. So off I went on wild goose chases, far from our claustrophobic booth, his killer breath and unwanted sexual advances.

The diamond runner role was one of bling retrieval. After Tamar had hunted down the requested diamonds of a certain color and grade though his labyrinth of shady connections, I play fetch. Good thing my SoHo walk-in wardrobe boasted a stellar collection of fabulous thick winter coats which could hide diamonds.

Discovering the deep bowels of the world of diamonds was eye-opening. I often found myself knocking on the doors of Hassidic Jewish lone wolves working in shoebox-sized offices with a touch of 'haunted house' vibes. These no-nonsense and non-verbal jewelers only responded to diamond requirements scribbled on paper. I'd give them my diamond wish list, and they'd pull out an envelope containing the required stones from a drawer. And of course, they'd hand me these things called GIA certificates - diamond passports, if you will. Then off I went to pick up other diamonds.

Talk about a fall from grace. So there I was, a diamond runner (which, by the way, doesn't even crack my top 1000 dream jobs). It was a gig that often left me feeling degraded and humiliated, but hey, it paid the rent for my tiny SoHo loft.

I had to turn my back on all SoHo fineries and dining. I ambled to Chinatown nearby which had its dark underbelly, for groceries and meals on a dime. The struggle was real.

In hindsight, I loved learning about the fascinating diamond-encrusted world that I was unexpectedly thrusted into. My knowledge of these shiny little rocks went from zero to a hundred real quick. I also found the one diamond that really stole my heart - the emerald cut diamond.

When the news of my visa approval hit, I was so happy I could have done a backflip. Anna was the first in the diamond district I broke the news to. Her reaction was a cocktail of emotions - she was thrilled for me, but also a tad blue about losing her top-notch friend and stand buddy. Unfortunately for her, she didn't have a ticket to escape her wretchedness there like I did.

I shared my joy with my new Ukrainian Jewish buddy, Mila. She's got this fascinating backstory, her Ukrainian Jewish family made the great trek to Israel after World War II. Fast forward a few years, she was drawn to NYC for a taste of that juicy Big Apple. Mila was working for one of the high rollers and her booth stared across from ours.

A beautiful, strong, bright, sparky, vocal and plucky woman, Mila is still my buddy and a mother of two beautiful children in Israel. We've always talked about a reunion and one day it shall come.

Well, the scoop also reached Micah, this drop-dead hunk who was a chip off the old block of a loaded Hasidic Jewish big shot with a massive booth next to ours. His father ran a well-oiled family business. Micah was a bit of a stand-up comedian, and we were each other's lookout. Little did I know then that Cupid was sharpening his arrow for us.

By the end of winter, I was iced-out of the icy-cold diamond district.

23

Micah

Micah popped my Hasidic dating cherry and also promptly planted the 'Please, No More Hasidic Dates' sign in my love life garden.

His deep-pocketed family originally hailed from Ukraine. Their journey took them from Ukraine to Israel, and then straight to the heart of the Big Apple, where they built a bigger empire of wealth. Boy, did they take a bite out of that apple. Micah comes from a large family - six siblings, all working for their dad like a well-oiled family business machine. Well, except for the youngest one who was only twelve and still trying to figure out algebra when I met Micah. Modern Hasidic Jews, they adhered to certain traditions from their religion.

His father runs a successful fine jewelry business, which, last I checked, is still ticking. A true businessman with a sharp acumen, he set up a big shop in the Diamond District and tapped on additional footfall at The Arcade with a big booth. The booth offered limited selections, but they were smart cookies, cross-selling all sorts of sparkly stuff from their main store.

Micah was the tireless runner bouncing between the store and The Arcade. On the days he was stationed at The Arcade, in the absence of his imposing and stern father, he was the life of the party, cracking jokes. Mila, Micah, and I were like the three musketeers of The Arcade. Mila's stand was right across ours. Micah's stand was nestled between us, like a pickle in a sandwich.

Micah and Mila were like a pair of fluorescent bulbs in the grim, windowless world that was Tamar. Mila and I would often hang out after work, sharing tales of the day. One day, she spilled the beans about their dating history. Turns out, they had a little fling back in the day. But it was short-lived because of Micah's strict family and religious background.

Micah exhibited two sides. On one hand, he was the picture-perfect Hasidic Jewish son. Quiet and obedient. Other times, he flipped to this fun-loving, cheeky, bright-eyed young man who loved a good joke. With his dark, devastatingly handsome features, you'd think he just stepped off a Milan runway. He was impeccably dressed in sharp suits. You could spot him from a mile away, shining like a diamond in the rough of The Arcade.

His good looks didn't go unnoticed as he was once strutting his stuff down the street when a Calvin Klein scout spotted him. As he was raised in a strictly religious household, he turned down the opportunity, forever to remain the most attractive man in The Arcade.

Micah's family remained a mystery to me during my time at The Arcade. They were mostly private, strict and religious. The men in the family didn't go for the traditional Hasidic side curls or Payos. Micah and his father were more GQ than Rabbi, favoring sharp suits over traditional attire.

The women in his family, they were a whole different ball game. They didn't swan around in wigs like some Ultra-Orthodox Jewish women do. Always in dark, solid-colored dresses, you'd never pick them out in a lineup.

The family kept to themselves at their booth and only engaged on a need-to basis, with customers and jewelers at The Arcade. Clearly the patriarch, their father cut a figure of authority and ran a seamless operation. He was the epitome of the strong silent type, doling out hushed orders to his clan. He was the only one who talked to the other jewelers. Obedience to him was apparent, and the family paid obeisance to him.

Micah asked for my cell phone several times. Not my number, but my actual phone. I surrendered it without thinking twice. Thinking back, I didn't know why I didn't question the request. Well minted, he must have had a few.

On the final day of work, a day I nearly broadcasted from the rooftop, I bade Micah goodbye. There was no response from him, and I simply shrugged it off. Oddly enough, a few hours later, we ended up in the restroom at the same time - talk about a weird coincidence.

Micah, who couldn't act his way out of a paper bag, seemed like he planned this 'accidental' meeting. The toilets were conveniently hidden from his family who were all camped out at the booth. He flipped the switch to his modern and carefree self and started gabbing away.

Micah: "Why didn't you call me?

Me: "What are you talking about?"

Micah: "I asked you for your phone and entered my number in there. I checked a few times and it's still there."

Me: ...

Micah: "I've been waiting for you to call me. I wanted to ask you out. I really like you."

Me: "I had no clue."

Micah: "Can I take you out for dinner?"

It wasn't anywhere near the Fourth of July but there was a firework show exploding in my ticker. The guy's confession hit me between my eyes - totally unexpected and a bit disorienting. And the cat he let out of the bag? It wasn't just any kitty. It was more like that crazy cat that ambushed me at my loft party, all claws and hissing. Playful but not flirtatious, Micah's overtures were never overt to me.

Love is both blind and blinding. Completely smitten, I overlooked all those tiny details that would eventually turn us into a romantic disaster movie. His religion, strict family, and the teeny-weeny detail that he wasn't allowed to date or marry someone outside his religion, well, that doomed us right from the start.

When I updated Tim on my love life, in true Tim fashion, he squealed, "Just have fun, girl!" Mila, on the other hand, understood the intricacies of Hasidic romances, having navigated those stormy waters herself, somberly rang the 'expectation management' bell. But alas, her words fell on my deaf ears.

A man of great style matched with great tastes, Micah picked a fine and splurge-worthy Russian restaurant for our first date. As if that wasn't enough to impress me, he completely swept me off my feet with a bunch of sweet-smelling roses.

Not a man of fiscal prudence, we'd be dining at the finest blowouts, and I'd be sipping wine all by myself as he didn't touch the stuff. Without the looming presence of his family, he was entirely a different being - sweet, thoughtful, romantic and gentlemanly. And when the lights went out, let's just say he knew his way around the bedroom better than Columbus knew the globe. His sharp humor stood out amongst his hefty list of great traits.

Cracks soon appeared despite the rose-tint that I refused to let fade. It seemed the family introduction chapter was ripped out of our love story completely, with me playing the role of the secret lover. Familial obligations formed the heart of his daily schedule. Fridays and Saturdays were Shabbat days with his family. He'd share tales of these elaborate rituals, but I was never on the invite list. Adding to the drama, he was the designated chaperone of his younger brother, escorting him everywhere like a secret service agent.

Fenced off entirely, I only knew about his family life as an outlier. Our moments together felt like scenes stolen from a romantic movie, sandwiched between his family rituals. At first, it was thrilling but soon turned out to be frustrating.

I had perceived a large age gap between Micah and his brother, only to find out that Micah was a baby-faced 18-year-old when we were dating. When he decided to come clean with his age a few months after, I was knocked senseless and speechless. Me, a respectable 27-year-old, dating a teenager? It was like a scene straight out of a sitcom. Never in my life then had I desired to be a cradle snatcher. It's a different story now, on a cheeky note.

Things began to click. He didn't touch a drop of alcohol because he was below legal drinking age. He was all about wining and dining me at steeply-priced fine dining but couldn't even get past the bouncer at a club. Soon, it grated on my nerves that I had become a Hasidic kept mistress. This whole cloak-and-dagger romance ran against the grain of what I stood for – openness and transparency.

Micah's family obligations ratcheted up. To juggle his time better, he roped in his cousin to be our chauffeur for our clandestine dates. Now, this cousin wasn't just any cousin. He was a real head-turner. An error of judgement made out of sheer desperation, he confided in his cousin about our hush-hush romance.

One evening, his cousin made a pass at me which was rebuffed. With his ego precariously dangling on a thread, he threatened to 'out' our relationship to Micah's parents. Everything came undone after that. We had to end us.

My heart splintered into a million little shards. Word on the street was, Micah's young beating heart suffered blows too. I had Frou Frou's rather aptly titled *Let Go* on loop, but stupidly, I wouldn't and couldn't let go.

Because of love, I was able to accept the hellish limitations exacted by his religion. To protect my fragile patched-up heart and inoculate myself from future heart breaks, I swore never to date anyone religious. I've never wavered on it. I learned to create a relationship rulebook, listing negotiables and non-negotiables, and I stuck to it. Religion remains a big, bold, underlined entry in my non-negotiables section.

24

I Spy with My Little Eye

Someone once tossed this gem my way: The best way to get over someone is to get under someone else. Pain nudged me to give it a whirl. While it holds little truth, traces of curation lie in believing that you're on the road to recovery, even if you're just taking a scenic detour through rebound-ville.

The gang added the Pan-Asian hotspot TAO restaurant and club to our epic weekend bar and club crawl. Suddenly, we found ourselves in the tight lines that wound around the block. This was the original TAO at 58th Street and Madison in Midtown. Owners and hitmakers Noah Tepperberg and Jason Strauss raised the bar and now they have an empire of big names like Marquee, LAVO and Vandal.

The swanky and eye-catching decor at TAO was like a magnet for folks who were just as glamorous and shiny. Men were incredibly hot. Now, it wasn't a queer friendly club with an open-door policy, but the inclusive gang included straight bars and clubs in our hit list, strictly for my benefit. Rarely did a night end without some hunky new arm candy on my arm or a fresh digit to save on my phone.

Then I started casually seeing Isaac, Mila's buddy from Israel. Just like the rest of us, he was trying to find his glittering opportunities in the Big Apple, by eking out a living in the Diamond District. As coincidence went, he was actually living in my old loft at Varick. And we never even bumped into each other when I was there. Anyway, he was just a few streets away in SoHo, which was super convenient.

A former sharpshooter with the Israeli army and a professional competitive shooter, Isaac was in prime shape. Adding to his charm, he had these sparkling blue eyes, and a face that was boyishly handsome. His golden hair was cropped close to his head, lending him a bit of a skinhead vibe. Violent he was not, but street tough he was, and working-class pride he possessed. The working-class ethos extended to his wardrobe – tough yet smart button-down shirts, pants and heavy work boots. Even though we were on casual terms, I introduced him to the gang, Kaylee and Jai. Before long, Isaac became a regular fixture at our loft parties.

Isaac had a cousin who he suspected was a Mossad agent. I trust you don't need an introduction to Mossad. For those who've been living under a rock, let me fill you in. It is the Institute for Intelligence and Special Operations in Israel and an elite spy agency responsible for counter terrorism, intelligence collection and covert operations. They are the second-largest espionage agency in the Western world, after Central Intelligence Agency, or CIA for short.

Most things covert like Mossad, MI6 and the French Foreign Legion intrigue me. I was dying to meet him, even though Isaac couldn't ascertain his agent status. As covert operatives, they're masters at concealment. Mossad agents are highly secretive and superbly-trained.

The opportunity to come face to face with a suspected agent arrived when he made an alleged business trip to New York one weekend. After the obligatory Big Apple sight-seeing, Isaac and his cousin dropped by my wild loft party. In the spirit of concealment, I concealed my enthusiasm at meeting him.

There he was, teetering on the edge of his 30s, with all the charisma of a cardigan. His expression was stuck permanently on polite. If the dress code was 'undercover in the sea of ordinary', he absolutely nailed it in his black button-down shirt and matching black jeans ensemble. But, at our raucous, rainbow-colored, flamboyantly fabulous LG-straight people party, he stuck out like a sore thumb, as he was the lone buttoned-up adult.

Well, there he was, glued to his seat, only interacting with Isaac, our resident drink-fetcher. I kept my eyes on him, like a hawk on a field mouse, tracking every lackluster move he made. All the while, I was waiting for him to slip up and reveal his secret agent identity.

All of a sudden, he jumped like a cat on a hot tin roof. Something was buzzing in his pocket. He dived his hand in and pulled out a blinking, retro pocket-sized pager. It was like a time machine to the days of boom boxes. If you're scratching your head wondering what a pager is, much like a boom box, do yourself a favor and consult Uncle Google.

Twenty years ago, we were all playing 'Snake' on our Nokia's, but pagers slide the timeline further back in time. We've progressed from the pager's one-way conversation, to the two-way communication of mobile phones. Although passé, it has withstood the test of time and still finds its place in hospitals because they're the trusty steeds in Wi-Fi dead zones. Encrypted pagers are less hackable than mobile phones, so confidential information remains, confidential.

Isaac's cousin squinted at the ancient pager, then shoved the relic back into his pocket. He scanned the crowd in the tiny loft, his eyes darting around searching for the elusive Isaac. Finally locating Isaac, he weaved his way through the crowd, moving with all the grace of a bull in a China shop. Isaac, possibly sensing his cousin's signals, looked up just in time to see him. His cousin leaned in for a few whispers into Isaac's ear.

Isaac caught on to my totally-not-obvious spying operation on his cousin. He scanned the crowd, found my not-so-concealed hiding spot, and shot me a secret look. Then he flashed a megawatt smile. I returned the grin, our secret agent code acknowledged. Just then, his cousin made a hasty exit, citing work as his reason for an early departure. We took his words at face value.

25

Have your CAKE and Eat it Too

As a card-carrying free spirit and liberal, I found myself getting my boundaries and personal values thoroughly challenged by the Big Apple.

Singapore is a small conservative country with a post-modern façade where women's rights exist. The Women's Charter legislative act was passed in 1961, but gender equality still drags its feet in the mud. Compared to the other countries with spotty records, we are in a sunnier spot, but it will take decades to tilt the scale fully into equilibrium.

I have no interest to dip into a lengthy socio-political discourse about gender and sexuality in my country. But I'll touch on the shocking headlines made in 1995, when a young Singaporean woman who chose the alias of Annabel Chong shocked the world by starring in *The World's Biggest Gang Bang*. She had sex with 70 men, 251 times, over 10 hours. It was a grinding, albeit short-lived world record smashed the year after. So much for the grunt work. Curiosity will lead you to google her story, so no need to get into the innings here.

The aftermath was seismic. A notorious porn sensation overnight, she brazenly challenged the sexual status quo of the country, and the world. To most Singaporeans, she put us on the world map of great shame and embarrassment. I never pulled an "Annabel Chong", but her story stuck on my mind and firmly defined my sexual perimeters. The question, "how far will you go?" loomed large in my mind.

The decade of 2000 stirred up a female sexual revolution and experimentation never seen in the city. Female empowerment flexed on *Sex and the City*. And leading the charge was none other than Samantha Jones. Unlike her three cohorts, Samantha Jones was a non-monogamous, man-eater with a voracious appetite for sex. She was the litmus test for the mainstream media to see how far they could go with overt female sexual explorations.

In the peak of this sexual awakening, CAKE decided to kick traditional sexual exploration out of the boudoir and into the hippest clubs around town. Co-created by feminist impresarios Melinda Gallagher and Scarlet Kramer, CAKE was an entertainment enterprise promoting female sexual empowerment through underground feminist sex and swinger parties in the city. Melinda is a sexuality professional with a master's degree in human sexuality and public health from New York University. Emily has a B.A. in women's studies at Columbia University.

I heard tell of these feisty, flirtatious, frisky underground parties, with everyone having their own tall tale about what went down. Apparently, the venue was always a big secret, revealed at the last possible second to drum up suspense. You had to be on an exclusive invite list or be a lucky plus one to get in. A secret password was required to get your scantily-clad self in. Speaking of dress code, you had to match the theme of the night. On swinger nights, you could be a voyeur or a participant.

These were hearsays. But one thing was clear. Every party was pushing the feminist sexual revolution envelope further. This wasn't your regular, filthy, boys-night-out that tilted towards men's take on fetishism. CAKE was a brute display of female sexual empowerment. We were in charge. We ran the show. I was entirely intrigued.

My lottery ticket to the legendary CAKE party came from none other than my semi-interesting date, Andy - a Turkish American who I met at TAO. No offense to Andy, but he was dull and lacking a certain shine. I was about to pull the plug on us, but then he dangled the tantalizing prospect of a CAKE party in front of me. Curiosity triumphed over guilt. I had to attend a CAKE party at least once in my life. It was a feminist rite of passage.

"School night" was the upcoming theme and sounded a disappointing note for me. Grapevine had it that CAKE parties involved few articles of clothing. I got the whole schoolgirl fetish thing, but it seemed like way too much clothing for a CAKE party. In keeping with the theme and aiming for a look between naughty and nice, I squeezed into a snug-fit, short-sleeved, buttoned-down shirt in white. I decided to give the top two buttons a day off, fastened the next two, and then tied up the loose ends into a cute knot. The finishing touch to my sassy schoolgirl ensemble was a short, plaited skirt in flaming red.

I was racking my brain trying to remember the name of the club where the party was held. But my mind drew a blank. My school days were long over but I squealed like a teenage fangirl when we slipped into the dark and intimate, velvet-roped club. The space hosted a stage, fronted by a small-ish dance floor where a body-stack of both genders moved erotically to the thumping hot basslines.

Ladies in the bloom of their 20s and 30s came dressed

to the nines, erring more on the cheeky side than the sweet. Some were arm-in-arm with men, while others were painting the town red with their girlfriends. Action was wholesome - kissing and groping. There was no gauche nudity, swinging or whatever goes but loads of sensuality.

More surprising fun and intimate revelry was found in the handful of dimly lit lounge rooms, that served as the main hubs for high jinks and hanky-panky. They were sparsely decked out with plush velvet sofas, for those who couldn't be persuaded to get off the couches. Debauchery kicked up a few notches there, and ran the steamy gamut from lip-locking, making out that stopped short of intercourse and private dancing. Interestingly, most of this sizzling spectacle was orchestrated by the ladies.

We ambled into a room buzzing with a private soirée. Here, a squad of screaming girls, who looked like they had the cash to blow, eagerly eyed and ogled a hunky golden-haired Adonis, who was stripped down to a red thong so tiny, it could've been a misplaced eye patch. Their faces were as rosy as the plush, velvety sofa they were perched on. From my vantage point, I could make out his rock solid tush. The sexier his dance moves, the harder the schoolgirls crushed on their heartthrob schoolteacher.

Then out of nowhere, the virtuoso performer twirled around and did a cheeky butt clench. It was our man, Joe. His washboard abs and bulging biceps were a dead giveaway. As soon as Joe's eyes locked onto mine, I froze like a deer in headlights, caught in a mental tug-of-war between the flight or fight response. After Joe had wrapped up his heart-pounding, not to mention risqué, performance, he strode over to me in his ridiculously sexy red thong that barely managed to keep his crown jewels in the treasure chest.

Joe: "Hey girl."

Me: "Hey Joe."

Joe: "Fancy seeing you here."

Me: "Yeah. It's my first CAKE party. Andy invited me."

Andy: "Hello. You two know each other?"

Big awkward moment.

Me: "Yes. Joe is a very talented dancer."

Joe: "Yeah, I've done a few dances for CAKE."

Me: "So lovely seeing you again, Joe. See you around."

As we escaped the pin-drop moment, Andy pressed me for all sorts of answers. I really didn't want to turn my fun feminist night out into one of lengthy interrogations, so I wrote Joe off as a dancer I'd bump into at a gay club.

We plonked ourselves at the bar, stage-adjacent. Over

drinks, I let out a sigh of disappointment that the party was as far from the debauchery-ridden extravaganza I'd heard about. Suddenly, up popped this brunette bombshell, decked out in a red lace number. She was wearing more hair than clothes, cascading waves of it down to her tiny waist, which she swished while performing a sexed-up dance.

"OMG Kimmie! Don't be a gawking tourist. Dance with her!" I could almost hear Tim's voice, laughing in my ear. So, I rocked my body, trying to match her rhythm. She pressed so close that I could see her pretty features and feel the squish of her ample bosom. Vacillating between a sexy-kitty-come-hither look and sweet, girly smiles, she had me giddy and enthralled. I cast my eyes down and admired her sun-kissed, toned human form. Andy was eating it up, getting a massive kick out of the whole performance. He was tossing me these "You go, girl!" type of nods.

When the music ended, so did her show-stopping gig. With her hand outstretched, she demanded $20 in an East European accent. I just stood there, rooted like a tree, mouth hanging open like a broken mailbox. Who knew we had to shell out for dances, even if $20 was affordable.

Andy plunged his hands into his pockets and unearthed a few crumpled notes. She watched, eyebrow arched, as he painstakingly ironed out each bill on his knee. And then, drama of all dramas, we were short of cash. Not wanting to shortchange a working girl, Andy played archaeologist again, this time unearthing a smattering of coins. I was ready to bury my head into whatever hole I could find. We cobbled together the payment, she shook her head and huffed off.

Clearly CAKE party virgins and amateurs, we found ourselves laughing at our own rookie mistakes. Then, from the corner of my eye, I spotted a fetching woman in her early 20s strutting across the dance floor like a runway model. Slim and fair with platinum-blonde hair that flowed straight and long, she was all decked out in a pink mohair crop top, so short the bottom of her enormous natural boobs peeked out. The top was paired with a cheekily short, pink and black plaited skirt that showcased her slender, alabaster legs.

I turned into a chick magnet, pulling in another round of grown-up fun. If we had to cough up cash for this one, we'd have to make a dash for those plush ropes at the exit. The dirty dancing began. Her moves weren't as silk and suave as the East European mover and shaker, but they were enough to hold my interest. And oh, Andy's too.

Moments later, she commandeered my hands and

placed them on her D-cup assets, hidden beneath her mohair top. I shot a glance at Andy who was busy playing his own game of peek-a-boo under her top. She guided my hands to explore the unfamiliar terrain of her well-endowed chest. It was my first expedition into the land of mammaries. My previous encounters had only been in the context of breast cancer self-checks - a far from erotic, more of a "dear-lord-let-there-be-no-lumps" kind. It was pleasurable that she used me to pleasure herself, while Andy pleasured himself watching the whole spectacle. It was a win-win-win situation.

She revved up her moan engine to max, then swooped in for a smooch. I felt her tongue dive into my throat. I nearly choked and my eyes nearly did a cartoon spring out of my head. Her hands moved swiftly across my body like a full-on invasion. Sensual, yes, but I tore myself away from her, much to her bewilderment. I nabbed Andy's hand, and we made our grand exit from the club.

That wild evening of eyebrow-raising exploration had me shouting from the rooftops - I am straight as a pole. That was the end of the litmus, or clit-mus test for me. As for female sexual empowerment, I certainly don't need to be at a club for that.

26

Oh Canada

It was time to swap my L-1A for an H-1B. An L-1A visa is an intra-company transfer visa, and a H-1B is an employer-sponsored non-immigrant classification which allows persons who are not citizens or permanent residents of the United States to work in a specialty occupation for up to six years, with very limited exceptions.

A visa was the holy grail for Tim, Claire, Sud, and every other adventure-seeking globetrotter who landed on America's star-spangled doorstep, chasing their dreams. The top three chatters of the gang were dating, sex and the coveted visa. Every Christmas, Tim wished for a green card through winning the great green card lottery, but the man in red wouldn't give it to him.

Just like the rest of the gang who got to the Big Apple before me, I developed an obsession with visa. I mean, my whole New York life pivoted on it. At first, I took it for granted as I got it easy. But then, when my L-1A was on the verge of being terminated, the thought of getting booted out of the country hovered over me like a pickaxe over my head. This unsettling fear permeated my New York escapade. I managed to lose it not once, but thrice. When I had it for the third time and then quit, I decided to give up the struggle, and head back home. I was done and dusted. The insecurity was unnerving.

Six months of visa limbo plunged me into penury. Not to mention a state of constant stress. Just because I found a company to sponsor my visa, didn't mean I'd get it. There was always the possibility of them rejecting the application. Warding off the sexual advances of bad breath flower killer probably took years off my life too.

There I was, standing on the precipice of my career taking flight. But first, I need to get my new approved visa. I had to exit the United States and scoot over to a US embassy in any other country. Down to my last cent, an air ticket home was off the table. So was borrowing. Tim and Kaylee were ready to offer loans, but the thought of being in debt felt like having a pickaxe over my head.

A quick jaunt over to our friendly neighbors in Canada was a fitting solution – wallet friendly, and yet to be crossed off my travel bucket list. Instead of flying, I thought I'd take a train from New York to Montreal. Since my last check,

Amtrak still runs a train daily from Penn station to Montreal.

More than an ordinary train ride, it's billed as one of the "Top 10 Most Scenic Train Rides in the World." The ten-hour ride is an unhurried visual feast through the lush wine country of Hudson valley, gorgeous green mountains of Vermont and other picturesque landscapes of Saratoga Springs, Ticonderoga and Lake Champlain. For me, it was a ride of a lifetime.

I have a soft spot for train rides. Slow, glamorous, swoon-worthy and romantic, they offer both outward and inward perspectives. Beautiful foliage, untouched nature and the constant change of pleasant scenery inspire quiet introspection. I once traveled through Europe by myself, doing a bit of soul-searching. Riding through routes that are inaccessible to other modes of transportation thrills me.

Then there's the allure of the train bars. Don't ask me why but I'm big on getting snacks from a modest onboard selection. A slow traveler but a fast drinker, I love feeling slightly buzzed on trains. There's magic in the mini wine bottles. I've guzzled down more of those tiny bottles than I'd like to admit while gallivanting across Europe. Plus, the train bar is like a secret club for interesting people who can chat your ear off.

Montréal charmed my pants off with her cobbled streets in colonial neighborhoods. More French than Canadian, her people carry around an admirable air of insouciance. I arrived smack dab in the middle of the Montréal Jazz Festival. We're talking world-class jazz line-ups here. My hotel was right across from one of the open-air concert venues. Coming from the whirlwind pace of NYC, Montreal felt like a breath of fresh air. My subsequent visa pick-up journeys took me further afield, all the way to Quebec City and Toronto. But, no matter how far I wandered, Montreal remained the apple of my eye.

On day two, I had a strange encounter. With a few years of solo backpacking experience tucked under my belt, I was no stranger to odd encounters.

During my introspective journey across Europe, I chugged from Salzburg to Zurich where I encountered an unfortunate incident involving a train conductor. I had boarded the earliest train at 6 AM and soon drifted off to sleep in a small cabin which I was sharing with an elderly lady. I was awakened by the sensation of someone close to my face. Upon opening my eyes, I was taken aback to see the train conductor's face nearly touching mine. He promptly clarified that he was just checking up on me. The cabin was devoid of any other passengers except us. Presumably, the elderly woman had disembarked earlier.

The conductor, pale, pudgy and not exactly eye candy, had merrily locked the cabin door behind himself before sitting next to me. His first inquiry was about my kissing skills, followed by the unzipping of his pants. Using his fat finger, he flicked his small and limp penis out of the slit in his boxers. I was taken aback by its unusually tiny size and couldn't help but take a closer look. Keeping my cool, I continued the small talk.

Me: "I'm an alright kisser. Haven't had complaints."

Conductor: "Would you like to kiss my dick?"

Me: "It's too small. There's nothing to kiss."

Suddenly, he rose to his feet, fastened his trousers, pecked my cheek, and murmured sweet words before exiting the cabin. The event didn't scare me, but it did leave me shell shocked. Reporting him didn't even occur to me, mainly because I doubted anyone would believe my side of the story. After all, it was my word against the train conductor's, without a lick of evidence.

Back to the strange encounter on my second day in Montréal. As an avid walker, I discovered the city mostly on foot. About a quarter into my journey, I got the feeling that I was being followed. Halfway through, my suspicion was confirmed. I had strayed from downtown Montréal to the greener pastures of Montréal Botanical Garden. It was quite a distance, and my feet were nearly done for. The garden was a real oasis, unlike any other I had seen, with a horticulture competition showcasing imaginative, colossal plant sculptures on display.

Feeling him drawing closer at one of the turns, I hid behind a green sculpture. Taking a quick glance, I spotted a young blonde man who had frozen in his tracks. Suddenly, I leapt from behind the sculpture, startling him immensely.

Me: "Why are you following me?"

Young blonde man: "I'm sorry. I thought you are cute. I'm Gaspard. I'm a tourist, like you."

Me: ...

Gaspard: "OK. I will not follow you."

He held his hands up, as if that was of any assurance. Face to face, I had the chance for a formal head-to-toe inspection of Gaspard. Pleasant looking and casually dressed in a T-shirt, sports shorts, and blue, dirtied Converse shoes that wouldn't hold up past that week, he emanated a backpacker feel. Slightly geeky and awkward, he came across as harmless and genuine.

Gaspard was permitted to stroll the city with me. I found out that he was in his early 20s and fresh out of a Parisian university. We spent the day engrossed in conversation. After several months of solo backpacking, he likely craved some friendly company. As someone who had also backpacked, I could relate the most.

As the sun went down, so did my guard. I welcomed him into my room, my intentions no more than sisterly camaraderie. His bashful, schoolboy demeanor was charming, and his fascination with me was evident. Unfortunately, the feelings were not mutual. We engaged in light-hearted banter over glasses of wine, the hours swiftly slipping away. Exhaustion eventually crept in, and we collapsed onto the bed in the most innocent of manners.

Montréal was a brief sojourn, and once I had my visa, my mission was complete. Despite Gaspard providing me with his contact details, I never reached out.

A few years ago, Gaspard found me on Linkedin, and we connected. He was still as schoolboy shy as before, and by then he was married with two children. This time, he asked for my number and spent over a year texting me to keep the connection warm. It felt like the same kind of infatuation he'd shown for me years ago, and I stopped responding.

27

The Intern from Panama

Speaking of pitches, I had to script a catchy description on the back of the book cover to pitch my story to you. If you're reading this, I probably have succeeded.

The stuff you snap up from shops, supermarkets, or even online can tell you a lot about how snazzy those brand or product pitches are. Unless, of course, you're the type of person who is magnetically drawn to the dirt-cheap, no frills, fun-free house brands. From the miracle serum you slather on your face, fully convinced it'll rewind time and smooth out those pesky wrinkles; to the thirst-quenching drink you reach for on a boiling-hot summer day, right down to your chosen sports apparel that screams your fashion prowess (or lack thereof) during your workout.

When you purchase a product, you're not just buying an item, you're buying into a story. The art of advertising is the art of the pitch, a dance between illusion and reality. There's no absolute right or wrong, true or false. Everything hinges on the clever positioning of a product. We don't just sell you tangible goods; we deal in dreams, aspirations, and benefits. Sometimes you fall for them hook, line and sinker. That is the beguiling allure of advertising - a power so persuasive that it lured me into its captivating realm.

My career in advertising spanned sixteen years and it elicited a mix of affection and antipathy in me. Some of the most challenging times in my life were during my tenure in this industry. I was exposed to the darker side of human nature through my interactions with advertising professionals. Regardless of the agency I was employed in or the part of the world I was in, I encountered the same charlatans exhibiting similar negative attributes. These included a veneer of confidence hiding deep-seated insecurity, cunning deception, a desperate urge to blend in, an inflated sense of entitlement and privilege, excessive self-importance, self-aggrandizement and an unhealthy obsession with power.

Pitching is the name of our game. If you, like me, are an aficionado of cycling, you might be familiar with a Tour de France adage – "You're as good as your last race." This saying rings true in the world of advertising too: you're as good as your last pitch. Don't get me wrong, not everyone in advertising is a bad apple. I have been fortunate enough to foster genuine friendships with individuals who uphold ethics and integrity in this dynamic industry.

These characteristics, arguably, are not exclusive to the advertising industry but are found universally. This was my belief until the TV show Mad Men aired, captivating nearly everyone with its witty narrative. Those who have experience working in New York's advertising sector would be able to recognize and appreciate the brilliance and relatability of the series. It seems some individuals in advertising, regardless of their location, tend to exhibit similar douchebaggery traits.

Mad Men is a pithy title with a double entendre - it's indeed full of mad men in advertising, and 'Mad' is short for Madison Avenue, where most of the glamourous advertising agencies were located. It was also where I worked.

Mad Men had been set in the 1960s, but the themes of self-identity, sex and gender roles, and old versus the young had permeated beyond the zeitgeist. Fast forwarding decades, the golden age of advertising depicted in *Mad Men* had been replaced by digitalization when I was working in advertising. Today, digitalization is upended by AI technology. Yet, interestingly, the politics in the industry remain the same. Advertising people don't change.

As Mad Men captivated viewers on screen, we were living our own contemporary version within the walls of the agency. Of all the global agencies I've graced, the New York advertising scene proved the most ruthless and cut-throat. Human Resources merely orchestrated hollow Punch & Judy diversions, while a pervasive 'Here today, Gone tomorrow' anxiety loomed over us like a dark cloud. The city was a swirling vortex of talent drawn from across the globe, all bristling with ambition, ready to snatch your job at the drop of a hat. I suspect this sense of insecurity persists today, the landscape largely unchanged.

In an industry plagued by sexism, women faced an extra challenge where gender equality was but a hollow promise. This was my personal struggle, compounded by two more - overcoming stereotypes associated with being Asian and non-American. These conflicts weighed heavily on me, causing me to unravel many times.

I contemplated if I should delve into the countless acts of unfairness and ceaseless criticisms I had to bear, such as the torment from the Fearsome Four at my workplace - a frat-pack trio consisting of the Creative Director, Associate Creative Director and Art Director. The fourth member is a D-cup bimbo Copywriter from the South who could barely spell. She had special privileges as she was banging the Associate Creative Director. She disdained me because I was Asian, a foreigner, and a threat to her. Consequently, I was subjected to daily mockery and ridicule. Remember the anxiety-inducing sensation of a pickaxe swinging over your head that I mentioned before? This was it.

So, here I am, deciding to jot down a hilarious little tale about our design intern from Panama. Isabel was one in a long line of creatively-challenged individuals who somehow manage to land internships in top-notch agencies. Her father was a prominent business owner in Panama with spidery connections that stretched all the way to NYC.

Isabel was a spry, 22-year-old bundle of joy and naivety. A fashionista, she'd strut into the office rocking a new hat every day. It was a breath of fresh air being the newbie in an office drowning in toxicity and politics. A common thread that ran between us was being foreigners, not from America. The Fearsome Four weren't too keen on that. But her internship had a three-month expiration date, and even the Fearsome Four could tolerate anything with an end in sight.

I took Isabel under my wing. We began with lunches

and soon, we were hitting bars. I wasn't sure if she had an appetite for LG-straight parties at my loft, I nonetheless invited her to one of my wild loft parties a few days shy of her return to Panama.

Isabel was chaperoned by her cousin, Javier, who spoke barebone English, so he became one of the bench guys. Before the party, I had given her a download of what to expect so she was super charged. She came armed with two bottles of tequila, and I eased her into the crowd by introducing her to the gang. Then checked in on her every now and then.

In no time flat, she became the tequila chick, dual-wielding tequila bottles like a cowboy in a spaghetti western, slinging shots that blazed a fiery trail down the gullets of the partygoers. She was clearly having the time of her life. An hour later, I did another quick welfare check. This time, gay guests were returning the favor, pouring rivers of liquid gold down her throat. The cheers were deafening - you'd think she was a circus fire breather.

At the witching hour of 2 am, Tim stampeded towards me on the rooftop and latched onto my arm. I nearly performed a full pirouette, abruptly ending my chat with a gaggle of tourists who, hilariously, had mistaken my rooftop for a sky bar. Tim's eyebrows arched and raised like two inverted v's that screamed panic. He blurted out, "Kimmie, you'd better come have a look. Your intern passed out, and the whites of her eyes are showing. It's scary!"

We bolted down the stairs to my loft. There, sprawled out on the floor, was Isabel. Javier dropped to his knees beside her, giving her a nudge. She was all whites of the eyes and twitchy moves - a scene straight out of "The Exorcist". As tipsy as we were, the sight of Isabel was enough to sober us right up.

"Quick, to the hospital!" I dramatically announced to the gathered crowd. Tim and I, clearly newbies to this medical mayhem, were left scratching our heads trying to figure out the next step. Sud, the ever-practical one, suggested we call the nearest hospital. Now, the real challenge began - navigating down seven flights of stairs. We ended up spread-eagling her, each of us clutching a limb, and began our slow and steady descent.

Almost jolted sober by the ear-splitting sirens of the arriving ambulance, we watched as two folks, who could've been EMTs or paramedics, we weren't sure, burst out of the ambulance. They promptly whipped out a stretcher. To keep things simple, and because I can't tell my EMTs from my paramedics, let's just call them EMT's.

EMT 1: "Are you the party host?"

Me: "Yes. We think it might be a case of alcohol poisoning. She drank a lot of tequila."

EMT 2 greeted Isabel with a swift ocular once-over, but she remained unresponsive.

EMT 1: "Is she your friend?"

Me: "Yes. This is her cousin. Her family lives in Panama."

EMT: "Alright. You and you come with us."

Javier and I suddenly became the "chosen ones". We were hurriedly shuffling towards the back of an ambulance. By then, we were SoHo's most sensational morning news with a large crowd gathering around us at the unholy hour of three in the morning.

Javier could barely piece together a sentence in English, but he was able to communicate his impending tragic fate, "My uncle will kill me." I shot him a look of sympathy. He didn't seem to be having a good time, and as the situation worsened, my empathy for him deepened.

As we hit the road, I found myself rubbernecking around the inside of the ambulance. It was my first time inside one of these metal beasts and boy, was it different from the movies. Alcohol ebbed and flowed into my consciousness. I squinted at the control panels near the driver. My bloodshot eyes landed on this black toggle with 'Wail', 'Yelp' and 'Hi-Lo' options. Intrigued, I gestured towards it and quizzed EMT 2, who was playing co-pilot, asking him to decode these options for me. He responded with the nonchalance of a seasoned pro, "They're just different sounds of sirens."

As the alcohol coursed through my veins, I found myself in a drowsy battle with the urge to close my eyes. In my slightly blurred mental state, a moment of clarity struck me like a lightning bolt - the sirens were eerily silent. Could this be your run-of-the-mill Saturday night teen alcohol-overdose run for the paramedics? Surely, just a routine pick-up, not worth blasting the sirens and adding to the city's cacophony. In the most innocent voice, I asked, "Can we hear the different siren sounds?"

My sincere request was met with a cold shoulder and complete silence. EMT 2 didn't even bat an eyelid at my question. Just as I was about to launch my question again, he flipped the switch from 'neutral' to 'Wail'. A piercing wail made me jump out of my skin and put me on high alert. Javier and I exchanged stunned looks. I broke into a mischievous grin. He was about to be condemned to death, and my fun was just getting started.

Hoisting my voice above the piercing wail, I belted out

a cheeky request - "Yelp!" EMT 2 sat there, statue-like, for a few heartbeats. The siren swapped its somber serenade for a jaunty jig. I chuckled hard. Now, I didn't intend to trivialize the situation, but I was so boozed up, and the fact that he was playing along was amusing.

"Hi-Lo!" I exclaimed, eyes twinkling with mischief. EMT 2, always the silent type, gave a solemn nod, accepting my demand. Immediately, a bubble of laughter burst from within me, spreading a contagious wave of joy around the ambulance. Javier, ever the stoic, tried his best to suppress the chuckles that threatened to escape his lips. He clamped his hand over his mouth. From dead man walking, he became dead man laughing.

We reached the hospital, where after a few hours later, the doctor informed us that Isabel was in the clear. Yes, it was alcohol poisoning, and they had her stomach pumped.

Crack of dawn, and there we were, scurrying off to her bedside. I wrapped my arms around her in a bear hug and planted a big smooch right on her cheek, the relief washing over me like a tidal wave. She was all set to jet off to Panama in a couple of days, kick-starting a whole new chapter. But first, she had some explaining to do to her fretting parents.

28

Alif

After years in the Big Apple, I became desensitized to the everyday sight of homeless people. They are multitudinous in the city and across America. These vagrants, vagabonds, tramps or whatever distasteful names they are referred to, are lost in a sea of anonymity. Their faces are often so soiled that they truly become faceless. Buried under the old, dirty rags that were once laundered, are destitute souls. Tragically, their entire existences are reduced to a few precious belongings they carry around. There isn't much to carry, not even hope. They fade into oblivion, becoming nothing more than public nuisances and annoyances. Such is the plight of the homeless.

Does the hackneyed plea "spare some change?" ring a bell? This is panhandling or begging for money in a public place. Unknown to many, panhandling violates New York's loitering law, Penal Law Section 240.35. On May 30, 2007, The New York Times, my top-choice NYC read, ran a story about a panhandler who valiantly fought New York's loitering law, arguing that it was as a violation of his free speech.

A year before his arrest for soliciting a dollar from a police officer, Eric Hoffstead began his life on the streets. Upon being arrested, he contested the charge through his court-assigned attorney, citing a 1992 federal law ruling that deemed such laws unconstitutional in New York City. However, despite this federal judgment, numerous arrests were still carried out under state law at that time. His petition was dismissed, and he was placed behind bars later for missing a court appearance. Although he was bailed out, he found himself back behind bars for trespassing at a public housing project. Hoffstead's story is a particularly striking example of the struggles faced by those without a home.

There was another. Alif had been the most extraordinary, and he was my favorite among the homeless in SoHo and beyond. I came up with a unique term just for him, a 'privileged homeless.' Despite being an oxymoron, it perfectly described his situation. He was well-received by some in the neighborhood and was granted several privileges.

In SoHo's more casual, less ethereal dining establishments, you'd often find Ali chatting away with staff or regulars at the bar. You might also see him picking at plates of complimentary food, gamely discussing politics, the day's news headlines or any other entertaining tidbits. He would usually wash his food down with free beer. The line between his sobriety and inebriation was so blurred, it was impossible to tell whether he was or not.

Despite his perpetual cheerful and friendly demeanor, he often encountered scorn and upturned noses from guests who frowned upon sharing a confined space with a homeless man. Nevertheless, the staff and owners of the establishments he frequented always treated him with respect. More often than not, he would head directly to the bar as soon as he entered. He never caused any disturbances or problems.

Alif had a presence that lit up any room he entered. He was a Black man, most likely in his 60s, with a lanky build and a slightly hunched posture. I remember his dirty black and white dreadlocks that grew thick like neglected tree vines. His skin sagged and wrinkled, resembling a beloved, well-worn leather bag. His face was generously freckled with black pigmentation. Dirt caked on his face and under his nails. His eyes, glazed over but sparkling with curiosity, were often the first thing I noticed about him. He had a voice that boomed across the room; you would hear him before you saw him. And if you were close enough, you could catch a whiff of his breath, sour with the smell of beer.

His broad smile revealed his few rotten teeth. The roots, clearly on their last legs, clung dearly to the pale gums. Once, he told me he was bound for the dentist as he was in immense pain from suspected cavities. It was a visit long overdue, and I jokingly questioned him on the need to go, given so few of the remaining teeth that barely soldiered on.

Alif wore clothes that were tattered and soiled, yet he held no crumpled cup for rattling spare change. He was not a beggar. Instead, Alif was a collector of discarded treasures, items once cherished by others but now abandoned on the streets. He found value in the forgotten, in the tossed aside. His chosen fragments found a new home in his black garbage bag, a makeshift vessel that he dutifully carried with him.

After years of residing in SoHo, I became friends with Alif. We frequently visited a few regular spots, with the noticeable distinction that I was a paying customer, while Alif enjoyed house privileges. One of my favorite places was an upscale Indian restaurant on West Broadway and Grand Street, conveniently located near my loft.

After enduring long, grueling days with the Fearsome Four at work, I often stopped by the bar for a few drinks or some food to unwind. Alif, a frequent visitor, joined us around once or twice a week. Alan, the restaurant manager, generously offered Alif two complimentary beers and a meal in return for his cheerful banter. Our evenings were filled with light-hearted conversations and jokes between the three of us. We purposely avoided asking Alif about his past or where he placed his makeshift cardboard bed, out of respect for his feelings.

One Christmas, before the gang arrived for our usual hungover Christmas huddle at my loft, I swung by the Indian restaurant to share some holiday greetings and grab a quick drink. I sidled up to Alif, who was parked at the glowing bar. I launched into a perky Christmas greeting. Alan lamented that he was unable to take a day off due to a shortage of staff. With Indian cuisine not being a traditional Christmas meal for many, the restaurant was mostly empty, except for a couple of bored waiters serving a few tourists.

I inquired about Alif's plans for Christmas, to which he gave a wry response indicating he had none. I hesitated to push him for details about his family's Christmas traditions, instead offering a sympathetic, "I'm sorry to hear" and diverting my attention to my drink, a Southern Comfort with a fizzing Sprite mixer.

With a twinkle in his eye, Alif shattered the silence, "Well then, gimme a Christmas kiss, China doll." The pet name 'China doll', though unoriginal, was what he had affectionately dubbed me. I shot him a blank look. My eyes darted to Alan who merely shrugged noncommittally. I was at a loss for words; was Alif serious? "Oh, come on. It's Christmas," he pleaded. I furrowed my brows in contemplation, my heart softening towards his request. "Alright, only one kiss, and on your cheek." I conceded. Alif's face lit up with delight, he clapped his hands as if he had just won a prize. Alan, meanwhile, took a large gulp from his beer, then set the mug down with a definite thud, his eyes gleaming with anticipation as if a spectacle was about to commence.

I puckered my lips, moving towards Alif with notable unease, hoping he had taken an extraordinary Christmas bath that day. I quickly pecked his cheek and immediately gulped down my drink. Alan and Alif applauded in response. I gave a swift salute before signing out and heading back to my loft.

One boring afternoon at the neighborhood laundromat, Alif ambled in, sporting his signature black bin bag full of his latest treasure trove, slung over his shoulder like Santa Claus on a budget. I stuffed the remainder of my clothes into the washer and initiated the wash cycle.

"China doll. I need yer help." Alif declared, setting his bag down on the floor near the counter adorned with highchairs. I hoisted myself onto a highchair, settling in for the expected 30-minute wait for the wash. "What's up, Alif?" I asked, my voice flat and emotionless. "I'm going to start a new business." he responded, his tone brimming with enthusiasm. "That's great! I'm happy for you. What kind of business?" I queried, my interest piqued at his announcement. "Moving van rental." Alif replied without a moment's hesitation.

My eyebrows lifted in surprise at the thought of Alif owning a vehicle, considering he was homeless. "You have a van?" I asked, my voice filled with skepticism. Alif confirmed with a simple "A'ight. I do now." Alif directed, pointing his skinny finger at a big brown van across from the laundromat. It was covered in a wild mix of spray-paint colors, like a failed graffiti project, creating a shockingly vibrant spectacle.

Alif gestured towards a cork bulletin board that was strategically placed near the washers. It was adorned with an array of DIY paper advertisements, each equipped with tear-off tabs. The board served as a community hub, a beacon of hope for those who'd lost their beloved pet friends. You simply attached a photograph of your missing pet to an A4-

sized sheet, scrawling your contact details on the tear-off tabs. Then, if your pet was found, someone could effortlessly tear off a tab and get in touch. The board also doubled as a marketplace, a platform for advertising services or products. Interested parties could simply tear off a tab bearing your number, providing a straightforward reference point.

"Can you create one of those for my moving van rental business?" Ali asked me politely. Turning back, I examined the vibrantly colored van again, this time noticing a UPS logo hidden beneath the chaotic splashes of color. Despite its faintness, I was able to discern it.

Me: "Alif, is that a UPS van?"

Ali: "Yes. I'm gonna borrow it for a few weeks."

Me: "Did you steal that?"

Alif: "Well, I wouldn't call it stealing. I borrowed it."

Me: "Alif, you can't do that. It's stealing."

Alif: "Fine, China doll."

A gentle giant known for his non-confrontational nature, Alif resignedly hoisted his hefty black garbage bag, whistling his way out of the laundromat. The UPS van, abandoned and mysterious, sat idle for days, drawing the curious glances of passersby until the authorities finally seized it one afternoon.

Alif had mysteriously vanished for several weeks. One evening, during my routine visit to the Indian restaurant for a casual meal and drinks, I found Alan on the verge of tears. Unexpectedly, he assumed the town crier role of Alif, and announced Alif's demise. I was engulfed by shock and sorrow, my eyes welling up as I gathered the courage to ask, "What was the cause of his death?" "Cancer," Alan responded, biting his lips to hold back his own grief.

Alan had more to reveal, pulling a neatly folded newspaper clipping from his pocket. He spread it on the bar counter, revealing Alif's obituary. I leaned closer, scrutinizing the vintage photo of a younger, unrecognizable Alif - clean-shaven, vibrant, and dignified. Underneath, a list of surviving family members trailed alongside a brief account of his illustrious legacy as a prominent city property owner.

Alan's eyes grew wide as he gave me several intense nods. I returned his stare, my eyes wide with surprise. We both had one burning question - who in the world was Alif?

29

Lights Out

"One of the largest blackouts in New York City history occurred on a hot Thursday afternoon, August 14, 2003. It is believed to have originated in Ohio, after a bush fire caused a transmission line to go out of service at around 2:00 PM. Within an hour, a second transmission line failed. These two incidents created a domino effect: one by one, overloaded transmission lines began to fail across the Eastern United States. To prevent an even bigger blackout, many power plants shut down voluntarily. By 4:00 pm, 3,700 miles of land affecting parts of Michigan, Ohio, Pennsylvania, New Jersey, New York, Connecticut, Vermont and Canada were without power. In NYC, all 11,600 traffic signals ceased to work. Policemen and volunteers worked together to direct traffic in major streets, but city streets remained chaotic. The MTA also shut down as a result of the blackout, leaving up to 400,000 people stranded in subway cars. People waited for rescue in stranded elevators. Fortunately, evacuation efforts began within ten minutes of the blackout occurring. Scarcity of cabs and an inoperable subway system forced thousands of people to walk long distances to get to their destinations."

Source:

"Disaster. New York City (NYC) Blackout of 2003." NYC Data, Weissman Center for International Business, Baruch College / CUNY 2021, baruch.cuny.edu/nycdata/disasters/ blackout-2003.html. Accessed August 11, 2023.

On August 14, 2003, Aya and I quickened our footsteps as we headed toward a meeting room at 4.52 PM. The creative team was about to present our creative ideas to a major client via a conference call scheduled for 5 PM.

I was paired with Aya, a Japanese designer, as part of a creative team. These teams typically comprise of duos, with a copywriter paired with a designer or a senior copywriter with an art director. They collaborate on concepts; the writer handles the copy, while the designer manages the design or art direction.

When tackling major pitches or briefs, our Executive Creative Director could mobilize several creative teams under the tutelage of a Creative Director. These teams, working in pairs, generate a wealth of innovative concepts. Afterward, they reunite with the whole team, including the Executive

Creative Director, who meticulously selects the top three concepts. If these ideas fail to meet business objectives or make the cut, it's back to square one. This is the dynamic, iterative process that fuels our creative operations.

Aya is more than a colleague, she's a dear friend. We collaborated on this book cover and related creative assets, despite the distance. The magic in our partnership is rooted in our understanding and camaraderie. We went through more thick than thin. I became thick while she remains thin.

After moving from NYC, I received annual Christmas cards from Aya, with pictures of her radiant family. I watched her two beautiful children grow on social media platforms like Instagram and Facebook. Originally from the Land of the Rising Sun, Aya was captivated by the shiny red allure of the Big Apple, prompting her move from Japan. There, she met her future husband, got married, and they eventually settled in bridge-and-tunnel Long Island. Sorry, I couldn't resist it.

I last saw her seven years ago during a demanding business journey to New York City. After my team meeting, she brought her children to my hotel room for a brief catch-up before I had to board my flight. Time seems to have no effect on her, as she appeared, and continues to appear, as beautiful as always.

On my premiere workday, Ben, the Creative Director, introduced me to my roomies - Aya, Jason, and Chuck. Chuck, by the way, was the one I mentioned earlier, banging the D-cup bimbo copywriter. Together with Ben and Jason, they formed the frat-pack trio. Add the D-Cupper, and you've got the Fearsome Four. Aya and I equally despised the creative team when their true colors shone. Despite her Green Card from her marriage, she, like me, was sidelined for being an Asian immigrant.

The moment I met Aya, she struck terror into my heart. The Japanese churn out some of the most legendary horror movies and she churned out some of the most legendary horror moves. Not long after Ben had exited the room, Aya, with an eerie calm, picked up a hefty hole-puncher from her desk. Without warning, she launched it with such deadly precision that it struck Jason squarely in the face. The impact was so colossal that the hole-puncher deflected off his face, crashing onto the carpeted floor with an echoing 'thud' that seemed to reverberate around the hushed room.

Chuck and I sprang up from our seats, our eyes first assessing the damage to the hole-puncher before shifting to Jason's injured visage. A stunned silence enveloped us. She continued her verbal assault on Jason with a blood-curdling scream. I was clueless his cardinal sin, but she clearly wanted his blood.

Aya was not one to be trifled with. Dubbed the 'iron lady' within the agency due to her fiery temperament, she had a no-nonsense attitude, caustic sense of humor, and was capable of piercing sarcasms that break down the most stoic. I was very fearful of her. When I was informed that I was to be her partner, I prayed hard for a heart of steel and the courage of a lion. Just so you know, when I told Aya I was going to include her in this book, she demanded to know which story she would be featured in. I have to admit, my knees turned to jelly a little. Yep, she's pretty potent.

Aya and Maggie Thatcher must have been cut from the same cloth, both having the softness of a cactus. But lucky for me, Aya decided to sheath her prickles around me after a few frosty weeks. We're like two peas in a pod, both Asian outsiders trying to navigate the treacherous waters of a highly toxic, political and gender-biased workplace and industry. We've got more battle scars than a gladiator at retirement. There was that one time when Ben saw us working late and inappropriately quipped, "Looks like an Asian sweatshop in here."

Do you recall the 'bitchy-bitchy' and 'peachy-bitchy' tags? Aya earned herself a shiny new tag – 'peachy-bitchy-bitchy'. I absolutely loved it when she vitriolically bitched about how vile the Fearsome Four were. Gradually, she began to show me her saccharine-sweet side. I understood that she needed to armor herself with a hard-shell façade not only to survive in the agency, but also in advertising. We got along like a house on fire.

Rewind to the conference room, August 14, 2003. 5 PM sharp, Ben, Chuck, Jason, D-Cup blonde, Aya, and I were all dialed into our call. Ben launched into his customary roll call, only to be abruptly silenced mid-sentence. Simultaneously, the room plunged into darkness as the lights and AC snapped off. The eerie silence of the room was tangible, punctuated by our uneasy shuffling as we grappled to comprehend the sudden blackout. Despite Ben's persistent attempts, the phone was as unresponsive as a doornail.

While we were in the meeting room, there was a flurry of activity outside. The soft sounds of moving chairs and chatter reached us. Chuck suddenly opened the door, and a cacophony of noise assaulted us. The lights outside were off, and we could hear people questioning what had happened. We instantly knew something was wrong.

From our lofty perch on the 76th floor of a skyscraper overlooking Madison Avenue and Grand Central Terminal, we were privy to a spectacular panorama. My gaze, however, was drawn to the glass windows of adjacent skyscrapers. A peculiar spectacle unfolded - scores of people, frantic, akin to ants aflame. Their heightened agitation hinted at an insidious unease. As I prepared to alert the team to this unsettling sight, the piercing wail of countless NYFD and NYPD sirens filled the air, reverberating down the avenues. Something was unmistakably amiss. Fear seized D-cup blonde bimbo, making her believe she was reliving the horrors of 9/11. We quickly left the room to assess the situation outside, finding a chaotic mix of emotions.

Visible distress painted the scene, with inconsolable tears flowing freely among some. Others were hastily packing their possessions, while a few stood stoic, hands poised on hips. Some retreated into solitude, sitting in chairs swiveled away from desks, immersed in contemplation about their next moves. Shock was evident on most faces, mouths agape in disbelief, while others cradled their heads in their hands, lost in profound thought. A veil of uncertainty hung heavy, the unknown future breeding fear that permeated the air, triggering a variety of reactions.

"May I have your attention, please? Remain calm. While we await further details, we know that we're experiencing a power outage that's affecting more than just our building. I comprehend the unease this situation may have caused and if you decide to leave, please do so in an orderly manner through the exit. Given that the elevators are down, be prepared for a descent via the fire escape stairs." Those were the reassuring words from our new Executive Creative Director, Helen Hogan, over the public announcement system.

The evident fear of a 9/11 recurrence deeply moved me. Jai and I were vacationing in Lombok, Indonesia, during the 9/11 event. I was quickly transported back to the chilling images I had witnessed on the news during that dreadful day. A live reporter was in the middle of her broadcast when in the background, thick black billows of smoke began to rise from the North Tower. It was a sight none of us would forget. Suddenly, United Airlines Flight 175 made its deadly descent into the South Tower. The reporter turned around in absolute horror, her tears mirroring our collective grief.

A bone-chilling fear seized me as I pondered our uncertain fate that afternoon. All communication lines were severed, leaving us isolated from our loved ones. Suddenly, images from the 9/11 footages flashed in my mind - papers fluttering in the air. Spurred by this, I dashed to my desk, hastily scrawling a heartfelt goodbye to my family, expressing my undying love. I tucked this precious note under my mug, hoping against hope that should the unthinkable occur, it would escape and flutter its way to them. It was a desperate, seemingly absurd act, but under the ominous circumstances, it was unquestionably worth a shot.

We picked up our bags and navigated to our floor's congested fire escape. Despite the crowd, the calm and orderly atmosphere eased our descent down 76 flights of stairs. The heat from the summer day was stifling due to poor ventilation. To lift the gloomy atmosphere, we cracked jokes and engaged in conversation. Aya stayed near me, unable to contact her husband but unfazed. Despite my fitness, I felt dizzy by the 50th floor. Others struggled greatly.

A crisis can reveal people's true character, and in this case, I was grateful to witness humanity at its finest. The crowd thoughtfully made a pathway on the right for those feeling unwell or needing a brief respite on the stairs. The ill were offered paper bags, food, and drinks which were collectively provided by the crowd. It was an exceptional show of solidarity, with everyone offering assistance and emotional support in every way possible.

In the whirlwind of the day's surprises, we totally blanked on the agency dinner at the nearby restaurant. Ben casually asked if anyone was still up for it. Someone threw doubt that the restaurant would keep the shutters up. But hey, if a terrorist attack happened, I'd want to die merry, well-fed and with a lethal drink in hand. "I'm in!" I hollered, setting off a chain reaction of party-ready peeps.

A whopping one and a half hours later, we finally stumbled across the finish line on the ground floor. Our mental reserves and physical strength were completely depleted. We staggered out of the building, hungry, thirsty and wearing our sweat like a badge of honor. Our dead feet still had to haul us away, as we needed to avoid loitering near the building entrance.

Defying our wildest imaginations, the scene that unfolded before us was far from apocalyptic; it was an event utterly beyond our imaginative capacities. The city that never sleeps was brought to a jarring standstill. Chaos reigned supreme on the streets, with vehicles frozen in a bizarre tableau of immobility. NYPD cars and FDNY fire trucks barreled down the deserted lanes, their sirens a jarring symphony in the eerie silence. The force of law was out in full display. Towering skyscrapers, now devoid of life, stood like desolate monuments while their inhabitants roamed the streets, directionless. The pulse of the city - public transportation - had flatlined, leaving everyone stranded. Everything we took for granted - cell phones, lights, electricity - had stopped working. It was a city held captive by an unprecedented crisis.

I peeped at my watch, it was ten past seven - time to embrace the unknown and indulge while at it. Barely energized, we trudged two blocks to the restaurant which seemed like a divine mirage amidst a desert.

The doors were flung open, inviting in the balmy summer breeze for ventilation. The sun, in its relentless glory, was still blazing even when the power lines had given up. We congregated around the owner, akin to pilgrims at a rest stop. As representatives of the agency, we introduced ourselves and began exchanging tales with him.

In the midst of a citywide blackout, the exchange of information was stripped down to its most rudimentary form - word of mouth. The proprietor, informed by his fellow F&B owners, was gripped with uncertainty over the duration of this power outage. As ice turned to water and his meats began to thaw, fear gnawed at him, a fear shared by many restaurateurs, that they might have to discard their food. In these dire straits, Ben proposed to proceed with our agency dinner, a proposal met with open, albeit sweaty, arms.

We weren't alone in our arrival from the agency, soon joined by an exhausted and sweaty contingent. Dressed in airy summer attire, we managed to endure the restaurant's warm, plush interior. As the daylight dwindled, it cast a glow on the polished cutlery, neatly tucked into impeccably ironed cloth napkins. Above us, elaborate chandeliers hung idle, relieved of their duties that evening.

Our feast was a spectacle of grandeur, reminiscent of a lavish last supper. The benevolent owner stirred ancient gas stoves to life and salvaged his dormant fridges. The banquet that unfolded could rival a state dinner, a dramatic turn from waste to graze. The opulence continued with a river of warm wines, iceless cocktails, and potent mixers. We indulged in every decadent dessert the house had to offer. As dusk descended, we were bathed in the warm orange glow of flickering flames dancing atop the candles, painting a picture of wax-dripped romanticism.

Every delightful journey has its sunset, and it was time for us to resume our voyage home. A few of us were merry, myself included, with my vision playfully doubling.

The feast had left us all buzzing with revitalized energy, ready to take on the world. However, the power was still down and public transport at a standstill. Aya and Stan, another Asian American colleague, found themselves stranded in the city, adding a twist to our tale. A quick plan was hatched. Aya and Stan would crash at my loft.

No sane person would choose to walk from midtown to downtown, but we unfortunately had no other choices. Alcohol managed to take some of the weight off my feet, yet it also turned me into a deadweight for Aya and Stan. They emerged as the true heroes of my evening, supporting me as my arms rested on their shoulders, and we tottered back to my place together. Move aside *Fellowship of the Ring*, this was *Fellowship of the Drink* in the making.

New York City, a vibrant metropolis, was suddenly swallowed by an unparalleled darkness. The city that never sleeps was now cloaked in a shadow so deep, it was like staring into an abyss. Streets filled with people, their faces illuminated by the soft glow of torches and candles, creating an eerily festive ambiance. The rhythmic pulse of hip-hop echoed through the vacant streets, as dancers transformed them into impromptu stages. Conversations sprung up, information exchanged, the atmosphere heady with surrealism. We journeyed through this bizarre night, occasionally checking street signs as we marked the passage of time in a city turned unrecognizably mysterious.

Two hours later, we reached my place, completely sweaty and more exhausted than ever. We enjoyed the revitalizing cold showers due to the loft's intense heat. We moved to my rooftop with cushions, pillows, duvets, and the mattress. Using these items, we constructed a makeshift bed. Jai sweetly checked in on us before returning to his loft.

Under the moon's soft glow, we lay on our new bed, enveloped by the night's darkness. The relentless network news helicopters cast a manic mosaic of light, punctuating our hushed conversation. We delved into our shared experiences in NYC - the good, the great, the bad, and the ugly, intertwined with our dreams of conquering the Big Apple. All these intimate confessions, whispered beneath the ever-watchful gaze of the shimmering stars.

After this incident, Aya and I forged a lifelong friendship. You can say that our friendship had gone through the darkest chapter of our lives.

30

Substance

I'm a self-declared shutterbug with a knack for finding the perfect angle for my food, cocktails, and holiday snaps. Now, I wouldn't call myself a pro (yet). I get my thrills from hunting down the best spots in town and sharing my finds - no pay, just passion. My Google contributions? A whopping 4260. That's reviews and photos of every joint you can think of. And get this - they've been viewed 11 million times as of October 13, 2023.

I caught the photography bug at the ripe old age of eight, thanks to endless hours spent ogling at Life Magazine in the town's bookstore. Fast forward two years, and my squirrel-like saving habits kicked in, helping me snag a special copy of Life 50 Years: Special anniversary issue – Collector's Edition. My favorite magazine was strategically stashed in the bathroom. It was my special treat during those lengthy toilet sessions, where I would lovingly leaf through the glossy pages filled with stunning pictures.

After eyeballing each photo, I'd sneak a peek at the captions to get the juicy, hidden tales of the snap. It's like playing a thrilling game of 'Perception vs Context' - my favorite adult pastime. One fine day, my beloved magazine simply vanished. My detective instincts led me straight to the prime suspect: Mom. When confronted, she confessed to tossing it out, mistaking it for some old, unwanted magazine. I went mental.

An avid book reader since young, I found myself increasingly drawn to the enigmatic world of photographs, attracted by their boundless capacity for interpretation. Where books appealed to my intellect, photographs stirred something raw and visceral within me. A beautifully composed photograph transcends mere depiction of subjects. It embodies the photographer's unique perspective, inviting you to explore the confined frame of their vision. Yet it also gives you the freedom to dissect and interpret the image as you see fit.

New York City was an absolute revelation to me in terms of photography. After all, it is known as the photography capital. Prior to her departure to America, Kaylee generously gave me her vintage Nikon FM3A camera, originally bought at a junkyard sale. Knowing my passion for photography, she thought it made for the perfect parting gift.

When Jai and I relocated to SoHo, my camera became my constant companion, capturing the unfolding kaleidoscope of fleeting moments in our new neighborhood. Each corner revealed a new scene begging to be immortalized through my lens. Each image told a story, together creating a personal tapestry of intimate creative encounters.

Back in my jobless days, you could often find me ogling at pictures at the International Center of Photography. I gathered a ton of breathtaking photography books for inspiration hits. I even got so swept up in the photography frenzy that I ended up turning a bunch of Wee Gee's monochromatic postcards into a shower curtain.

Time was on my side again. The agency laid me off, freeing me to immerse myself in my artistic endeavors. When human resources delivered the news, my fury couldn't be tamed. I stormed into the office of the new Executive Creative Director, Helen Hogan's office, demanding an explanation. I had tolerated the Fearsome Four, a gamut of injustices, humiliations, and bullying, because my visa status was contingent on my employment with the agency. The notion that everything I had worked for could be uprooted and snatched away by a decision was profoundly disconcerting.

My life was once again turned topsy-turvy, at a drop of a pin, and I wanted to know if the decision was made on a whim.

I lugged along my work, the list of awards I had won, and my portfolio as proof of my worthiness to my position at the office. Then came the moment of truth, without the sugar coat. "Look, we needed to make deep cuts. This is simply how business operates. "You're top on the list because you're unmarried, without dependents to care for. You're neither American nor Jewish," she said. I was dumbstruck, my eyes wide and mouth agape. The brutal truth landed like a punch, right between my narrowed eyes. It was served to me cold, without an ounce of sympathy.

In the current climate of 'Woke Culture,' her words would have led her straight to the corporate guillotine. At that time, I was oblivious to my rights – or if I even had any. Today, the 'Woke Culture' might have masked the ugly reality, wrapping it up in a prettier package. Each word she uttered resonated deeply. Already facing discrimination as a non-American, Asian woman, I wondered, what's a few more? To them, I was nothing more than another casualty.

Once more, my life was thrown into chaos as if the rug was yanked from beneath me. Finding myself at the juncture of remaining or departing, the thought of enduring the grueling process of job hunting, visa application and the prolonged wait for its approval, all while staying financially stable, was overwhelming. My finances had just recovered, and I was about to bleed my coffers dry again. The thought of surrendering my vibrant life in New York City seemed too simple a choice.

My love life was as barren as a desert. I spent all my waking hours working and my few sleeping hours working on sleep catchup. I resolved to inject some passion into my life. Exhausted by the monotony of meeting carbon-copies of men in the city's nightlife, I turned to Craigslist, on a quest to find a man of depth and substance.

If you've ever lived in America, you're likely familiar with Craigslist. Unknown to you? Give it a quick Google. This online platform has it all: job listings, housing rentals, service offers, and even a dating platform long before the era of Tinder and Bumble. My personal favorite? The 'Missed Connections' section – a unique space to reconnect with intriguing strangers you crossed paths with but never got the chance to meet.

As an exaggerated example, imagine this scenario: You were at the Canal subway stop, waiting for the N train en route to 34th street. A strikingly attractive gothic woman caught your attention at the platform. You both exchanged smiles, and a few minutes later, the train arrived. She boarded the train, but you didn't. Unexpectedly, you were tripped by a subway busker who was dragging a massive cello across the floor. You looked up, and to your dismay, the train doors had closed. The train departed, taking the girl of your dreams along with it.

In an attempt to reverse the sliding doors of fate, you put up a post in the 'Missed Connections' section on Craigslist, hoping she would stumble upon it and reach out to you. As luck would have it, she does. You both connect, and your story takes a turn for the better, culminating in you both living happily ever after. This is just a made-up example of many fascinating posts found in 'Missed Connections.' Some of them were so hilariously absurd that I had spent hours reading them purely for entertainment.

Once a useful platform, Craigslist quickly developed a dark reputation as a hub for fraud and potential danger - a reputation immortalized by the chilling Netflix film, "The Craigslist Killer." This film reveals the sinister double-life of Philip Markoff, a promising medical student turned brutal murderer, who found his victims through the platform. The underlying message? Craigslist has been infiltrated by weird individuals. Similarly, Tinder has its own dark narrative. The true crime documentary, "The Tinder Swindler," tells the tale of a deceitful fraudster who used the dating app to swindle unsuspecting women out of their money, providing further reason to swipe left on the app.

So, there I was, trawling Craigslist and I bumped into James - an Irish clicker, a witty and stylish photographer in his 30s. He was a creative soul with a love for arts and culture. I'd never dated a photographer before, so it was fab to gab about F-stops and compare creativity. James was an exceptional photographer, but like most things in the city, photography is another brutally competitive terrain, which sees the best contenders from America and the world, all vying for money and glamour.

His craft had to wait as he first had to make ends meet as a photographer's assistant. Not just any photographer, but a hotshot fashion photographer who had fired out iconic images for all the top glossy fashion magazines. When he dropped the name of his boss, my jaw hit the floor. The fashion world, so alluring yet aloof, was suddenly within arm's reach.

Oh, the life of a photographer's assistant, you ask? They're the superheroes behind the scenes. They help conjure up shoot plans, magically ensure all gear is on point, and are always ready to dive into any impromptu tasks the photographer might toss their way. They help keep the camera rolling and the creativity flowing.

Over time, James became increasingly frustrated. Being the assistant to a famous photographer, who we'll sneakily call Philippe, was like being his bitch. Philippe, when he was behind the lens, was a total diva – flighty, capricious, moody and extremely volatile in his temperaments. Not only did Philippe have exacting standards in photography, but he was also unreasonably exacting on his staff too. James had to dance on hot plates to keep up with Philippe's whims and fancies. His life became a never-ending marathon, often causing him to bail on our romantic rendezvous at the last moment. He was like a puppet, his strings pulled by the ever fluctuating mood of Philippe. This led to us playing an exhausting game of relationship ping-pong, breaking up and making up again and again.

One time, James wooed a post-break mend with a dazzling invitation to a private party. It was with Philippe and his crew, at one of the hottest and most celebrity-soaked clubs in NYC. This club was completely out of my league, and I longed to go. So, I put on my game face and said yes.

I arrived fashionably late and gave them some wiggle room for their little team huddle. While waiting for James at the club entrance, my excitement ratcheted up as I saw film, fashion, socialite, model and arty types revolving through the door. Once we breezed past burly bouncers, the club's exclusivity hit me - just a handful of tables nestled among palm trees and lavish sofas, with nary a dance floor in sight.

James introduced me to Philippe - the human embodiment of a sun-dried tomato with wrinkles to match. His hair was a jazzy mix of black and white curls, slicked back with gel. Dressed in a black blazer, button-down shirt, and matching trousers, he could've been easily mistaken for an accountant on a break rather than a famous photographer. His signature unibrow may resemble a dramatic theater curtain, but it's all part of his mystery. When we shook hands, his lips curled into a knowing smile. Then he sat back to silently marinate in the ambiance.

A sizzling, leggy, blue-eyed blonde model was nestled within our group. Her slender legs seemed to stretch out for miles, forcing me to navigate around them carefully to avoid an embarrassing tumble. We shared air kisses and with a flirty flick, she adjusted the straps of her saucy little black dress, revealing just a tease of her generous cleavage. "This is my boyfriend Marcel", she purred, her words draped in a rich French accent. Marcel was charm's antithesis, draped in a garish flamingo shirt that only amplified his plumpness. His attempt to look cool with those massive sunnies was quite the comedy show. I had to swallow a giggle - it wasn't the night to embarrass James.

There was no warming up after the icy introductions. James, the ice breaker, broke the awkward silence with news that three of his merry crew fled the scene an hour earlier. So, suddenly, just like that, it was down to us. I wasn't vibing with them and felt sorely out of place. The music was thumping away at a decent decibel, but no one was making conversation. Philippe, he was off on his own little space mission, mentally orbiting some distant planet.

Action then made up for words. The blonde model gently nudged a shiny silver tray towards me. On it, a thumb-sized white powder hill and four little powder roads. A curiously coiled Benjamin and a credit card joined this peculiar party. It felt like a quirky ritual I had to go through to bond with the lackluster group.

Well, here I was, face-to-face with a moral conundrum. Drugs? Not my scene. My only partner in crime is tipple. Dialing up the pressure by a smidgeon, James leaned in and whispered, "Do a line."

Cocaine was unchartered territory for me. Sure, I've seen it on TV, but my nostrils were strictly for breathing. How does one even partake? I was in a pickle – outing myself as a drug newbie wasn't an option. And it's not like I could sneak off to the loo and YouTube a 'Snorting Cocaine for Dummies' tutorial. This was pre-YouTube era. As I gazed at the tray, the group grew restless, waiting for my internal Shakespearean monologue to wrap up.

Putting aside my internal freakout, I leaned towards the sleek tray on the table and saw my awkward face staring back at me in its shiny surface. I gingerly picked up the rolled-up Benjamin. Anxiety rose up like a tidal wave and a surprise cough sprang out, catching me off guard. I turned the scene from a gritty crime drama to a magical fairy tale, blowing the lines away. The powdery substance danced in the air, twinkling like fairy dust under the club's lights. A collective gasp echoed around the table.

"Oh my god, I am so sorry. Oh my god, I am so sorry. Oh my god. I am so sorry." I babbled, repeating the phrase over and over like a glitching robot. What was the street value of the pixie dust I just blew away? Was there a prison sentence for being a bumbling fool? I felt like a clown in a sea of sophisticates. James could not have agreed more. With a swift and decisive movement, he pulled us both up, muttered an apology to the shocked audience, and whisked me away from the glamorous party, where I had performed like an "F-grader" trying to fit in with the "A-listers".

I was reluctant to end my relationship with James because I thought he was a man of substance. But I really blew it. Literally. I blew white powdery stuff off a tray, and well, our love story took an interesting turn.

We mended fences, but the real finale was a Halloween bash where I became Svetlana, a feisty Russian lady of the night. Blonde wig, Russian accent, the works. Unlike a true Russian, my vodka tolerance was pitiful. We both got liquored up and quibbled over the same tired issues. James sent me home in a taxi. Picture this: me, with the windows down, trying to keep my stomach contents to myself and not lose my blonde wig to the wind. I'm pretty sure I gave the onlookers quite a show.

The following day, I was nursing the mother of all hangovers, and I couldn't help but connect the dots back to James. That proved to be the final nail in the coffin. Substance, no substance, I was done with him.

31

Another Reality

In the bleak weeks following my layoff, my motivation plummeted to nonexistence. My days devolved into a monotonous cycle of mindlessly watching MTV reality shows and aimlessly browsing Craigslist. These distractions served as adequate narcotics to numb my senses. I fell from grace, from a fashion-savvy, boutique-hopping diva in SoHo, to PJ-clad homebody and nobody, trapped in her SoHo loft. MTV reality shows like *The Osbournes*, *Punk'd* and *Cribs* whisked me to a realm of reality where I was a passive gorger of thrashy content. For the record, I've never been a TV person.

Let me tell you about my new favorite sitcom, "Keeping Up with Cesar." Work soaked up so much of my time that the loft was turned into a crash pad. But now, homebound and bored, my building superintendent became my daily dose of entertainment.

This tiny, wrinkly, septuagenarian from Cuba was a sight to behold. With a pixie-like face and cataracts so white,

I often wondered if he was moonlighting as a blind man. Don't let the frail frame fool you, this guy had style. His daily uniform? A flat cap and the kind of Hawaiian shirts tourists buy thinking they've gone native. Despite his age and brittleness, he handled building chores like a champ. It was a spectacle more impressive than any reality show could offer.

I had strutted past his ground-floor grotto a gazillion times, but one day, my nosy nature nudged me to take a peek. Holy hoarders. The place was stuffed to the rafters with ancient relics and dust-bunny colonies, all carefully curated over eons. A skinny pathway, barely lit, snaked through the clutter, kind of like Dorothy's obstacle course to Oz. Except here, not even a desperate Dorothy would be clicking her ruby slippers, chanting, "There's no place like home."

Cesar's lips were sealed tighter than a clam with a pearl when it came to his backstory, which added an extra dollop of mystery to his persona. An early bird, he was hard at work by 6 in the morning. Come 11 a.m., he'd march to a derelict and abandoned storefront across my street, which served as the stage for his daily Cuban symphony. Armed with a band of silver-haired, Cuban gents, they'd strum, pluck and sing their hearts out, transforming the dilapidated store into a rich tapestry of Cuban culture. From my lofty perch, I had a personal, front-row seat to these heart-tugging, salsa-dripping performances.

Cuba's got this crazy mix of music that's a cocktail of Latin American, North American, African and European beats. Cesar once confided in me, mid-cork-popping of a Cuban wine bottle his son shipped over like clockwork, that they weren't just playing for pennies. It was a social club for them, a clubhouse of chords. Funny thing is, the roots of Cuban music trace back to cabildos, social clubs of West African slaves. The next day, I watched their gig with new eyes. They rocked Cuban American jazz with a reckless abandon that was free and liberating.

I got sucked into an alternate reality via Craigslist, becoming a social games maestro. The absurd content found on the platform had me hooked and soon, I was addicted to hysterical posts on 'Missed Connections', 'Rant and Raves' and 'Dating'. There were bored souls who tossed out ludicrous baits in anticipation of snagging an unexpected catch. For example, John Doe who worked in midtown, had had his fill of lonely lunches. He put out an ad, searching for a no-strings-attached lunch buddy to fill his lunch hour.

There were also double-lifers – these could be unsuspecting, ordinary people who might be standing next to you on the subway, or a high-powered executive calling the shots. These individuals harbored deviant streaks and fantasies that Craigslist allowed them to express. Some of these deviants teetered on, or crossed over into, criminality, such as the infamous Craigslist killer, Philip Markoff.

The audience pool was a neat dissection of our society at large - cheaters, criminals, shady and seedy people. Not to mention, a subset of sexual deviants who were into fetishes and sexual kinks.

Even within the darkness, there was light - authentic individuals seeking something quirky, fueled by curiosity to explore how the platform could satisfy their hidden desires. My alignment? The latter. Am I a deviant? Yes. Deviance fascinated me during my Sociology studies. I'm a non-conformist with a strong distaste for monotony. Always inquisitive, yet fervently distancing myself from sexual deviancy or criminality.

From a passive reader to social games creator, I toed over the line with my inaugural test post, "It's a cold winter evening and all I want is some warm and friendly company. Can someone head over with a bottle of fine wine?" And then, boom shake the room. Close to a hundred replies tumbled into my email, within an hour. It was like I'd just downed a triple espresso shot. Suddenly, I was the ringmaster of my own digital circus. Did I continue with it? Hell no. But my brain gears were spinning like a hamster on a wheel. So I decided, why not crank up the fun factor?

My first audacious social game? Massage by the non-masseuse. I found myself perusing listings in the now-extinct 'Services' category, a relic of days past, when I stumbled upon a flourishing sub-category of massage services. These ranged from the steamy and sensual to the therapeutic and healing. Different strokes for different folks. Then, a light bulb moment. What if I create a new category of massage services, one which was performed by an untrained neophyte? Transparent that it was intended to be a social game, I appealed to anyone who was keen on getting a non-sexual massage using rubbish techniques. An hourly rate applied, as compensation for my time.

Boom. My inbox was suddenly swarmed by a tsunami of testosterone-fueled replies. Sifting through the barrage of saucy solicitations, I managed to salvage five non-raunchy, sincere messages. I quickly whipped up a rule book, shooting it over to my chosen five. As they obediently agreed to my terms, I felt a strange power rush - was I running a secret BDSM lair? Safety concerns? Nah. That was why I spooked out when I read about Philip Markoff. That guy's first victim was a masseuse. What were the rules?

1. Communication is prohibited during the service and no questions were to be asked, except in relation to time and requests to stop the service.

2. No sexual requests or touching of the non-masseuse.

3. There must be a show of respect for the non-masseuse, by bowing before and after the service.

4. The client is responsible for booking and paying for a room in a reputable hotel, ensuring a safe and comfortable environment for the service to be delivered in.

5. The client will wear clean, loose-fitting shorts to maintain hygiene and ease during the massage.

Did I continue? You bet. The silly extremes folks reach for their kinks had me in stitches. Many times, I barely kept my giggles in check while providing services. Oh, the thrill of power when I was at the helm. They must have gotten fetish kicks out of playing by the rules.

How did I pull off a massage without knowing any techniques? Well, I kneaded, pounded, and traced alphabets on backs like a preschooler learning the ABCs. Sometimes, just for giggles, I'd go one-handed, leaning on the other like a bored painter. An hour was my limit though, any longer and my head would've popped from sheer monotony.

Out of my small troop of obedient clients, one really stood out - a towering, distinguished corporate honcho of an average build, likely marking his early 50s. A man of luxury, he opted for a posh hotel smack dab in the middle of the city. He swanned in, exuding CEO vibes, dressed in a slick suit and tie. He was as polite as a royal butler, a total gentleman, and treated me with the utmost respect. As he changed in the bathroom, his work ID played peekaboo from the pocket of his swanky designer bag. Curiosity got the better of me and I sneakily took a gander at his name and the big-shot bank he worked at.

Despite my crappy service, he tipped me a cool $100 and said I could have the room to myself for the day. He plopped the card key on the table and left. After a bit of online snooping at home, I discovered my mystery client was a big-time CFO at a well-respected bank. I could not decipher why he'd want to become a gambit in my game.

The first audacious social game was such a riot, it paved the way for a sequel. Enter 'Rent-a-Friend' - for those who fancy the idea of hiring a pal for an hour or two. Maybe you needed a +1 for a swanky soiree, a dinner date, or a pal to share popcorn with at the movies - the reasons were as many as stars in the sky. When I threw conversation into the mix, the dynamics changed. Sure, there were rules to follow but I retained my grip on power. A new thought was introduced – would you bare your soul to a rented friend, knowing you might never cross paths again?

I posted a bait ad and, boom. My inbox was suddenly swarmed by a tsunami of testosterone-fueled replies. Sifting through the barrage of saucy solicitations, I managed to salvage five non-raunchy, sincere messages. I quickly whipped up a rule book, shooting it over to my chosen five. If this sounds familiar, that's because the responses were as predictable as a rom-com ending. What were the rules?

1. It's not a date. It's a friendship.
2. No sexual requests or touching of your rented friend.
3. The client will suggest an open venue for the meet.
4. The client shall pay for all expenses of the meet.
5. The client will be decently and respectfully dressed for the meet.
6. The client has to exercise utmost respect towards the rented friend.
7. Your rented friend reserves the right to refrain from answering personal questions.

8. Friendship ends when the service ends.

My adventures in client relations could fill a novel, but let's focus on a couple of standouts for now. One errant client and I met at a dive bar in Alphabet City. We were having a fantastic chat, bonding over our shared interests, when all of a sudden he suggests we extend our tête-à-tête past the agreed time. That was already a no-no, but then he had one too many and tried to kiss me. I quickly stepped back, reminding him of the rules, but that seemed to have flipped his switch. Not one to accept bad behavior, I decided to make my dramatic exit. As I walked away, all I could hear was his colorful vocabulary.

I broke rule 8 when I met Adam. He was both a gentle man and a perfect gentleman, possessing a heart of gold that drew me toward him instantly. Adam, a master at making a woman feel cherished, secured a highly coveted table at The Blue Ribbon Brasserie in SoHo, one of my preferred dining spots. His chivalry didn't stop there; he also gifted me a fragrant bouquet of roses, presented in the sweetest way possible. Despite being touched by his sweet gesture, I had to reiterate rule 1 - this was not a date. In a soft voice, he acknowledged this, stating he simply wished to make me happy.

Like everyone else, I probed his motivation for answering

the ad. His response, tinged with shyness, was that he had always yearned for the extraordinary experience of sharing a Blue Ribbon Royale with a stranger at the renowned Blue Ribbon Brasserie.

The Blue Ribbon Royale, an item that remains a fixture on the menu, is an impressive tower of fresh, cold seafood that never fails to draw gasps of admiration from onlookers as the waiter parades it through the restaurant to its ordering table. The variety of seafood on the platter is as diverse as the life in the ocean - raw oysters, New Orleans shrimp, ½ chilled lobster, shrimp and crab cocktail, caviar, clams plus two shots of chilled vodka. "That's all?" I asked. "That's all," he replied.

In Adam, a fellow creative, I found a dear friend. His talent for mandala art left me speechless, and I was often a guest at his art shows. His patience was a wonder, mirrored in his intricate work. From a simple 'Rent a friend' client, he evolved into a cherished presence at my loft parties and museum visits. Our bond was purely platonic; his gentle spirit was a joy to be around.

Years later, Adam moved to Thailand. Our friendship remained strong despite the distance. One day, he emailed me with joyous news - he was becoming a father with his Thai girlfriend. This surprised me as I'd always perceived him as asexual because of his gentle demeanor.

In 2016, my heart shattered as I read about Adam's passing on my Facebook feed. He was taken from us by a swift and undetected lung cancer. The news of his departure hit me hard, yet I found solace knowing that his memory thrives through the heartfelt birthday wishes, beautiful remembrances, and tender words from his family and friends, still being posted on his Facebook profile. A pang of regret still hits me; I never had the chance to bid Adam farewell, his departure was just too sudden.

Farewell, dear friend. Your incredible art, beautiful heart and gentle ways live on with me forever. I appreciate our time spent in the Big Apple. You taught me much. Thank you for your friendship. I hope you are in a good place because you deserve to be.

32

The Year-End Bonus Drink Challenge

December unequivocally crowned the busiest, most exhilarating month for the gang. We reveled in build-up-to-Christmas loft parties, stepped-up gay and straight bar and club hops, extended Sunday nurse-your-hangover brunches, the annual Christmas and Welcome-the-new-year-with-a-big-bang loft parties. Notably, Tim and I spiced up the year-end routine with his company's annual party, featuring the notorious company bonus drink challenge. We started each challenge looking pretty and ended, pretty wasted.

Tim, the number cruncher extraordinaire, was an accountant at an ultra-conservative insurance company. Now Tim, like many of our fabulous friends in the LGBTQ+ community before the 2020 great gay awakening, kept his true colors under wraps in his early years at the company. Risk of homophobic backlash and discrimination kept him huddled in a metaphorical wardrobe. There were whispers, but you didn't want to throw anyone a bone of certainty.

So, in my bag of roles as Tim's buddy and fag hag, I was also bestowed the honorary title of "pretend girlfriend". As the clock was ticking down to his company's grand annual party, I was drafted into service as his sexual orientation decoy. I tried to level with Tim that there was a snowball's chance in a sauna that anyone would buy that he wasn't as gay as a rainbow unicorn. Tim's more in touch with his feminine side than I am. From his flamboyant chatter to his sassy strut, there's about as much heterosexuality in him as there is in a feather boa. The joke was on us, but I was more than willing to play along.

On the evening of the much-anticipated office Christmas party, Tim and I rendezvoused in the lobby of an astonishingly "meh" four-star hotel. Unbeknownst to us, we were about to transform into the Bonnie and Clyde fashion outlaws of the evening.

There was Tim, strutting into the party in his flamboyant gay uniform, contrary to his belief that he had dressed the part of a straight man. His shirt was so tight it was screaming for mercy, the buttons straining to hold in the sheer power of his pecs. His pants, a pair of skintight masterpieces, clung to his thighs like a stage-5 clinger on a second date.

"Women who wear black lead colorful lives," Neiman Marcus once said, and those words stuck to me like glue on glitter. Black rules my wardrobe like a stern, fashionable monarch. There I was, on a night grander than a royal ball, adorning myself in a black PVC sleeveless top that hugged my figure like a second skin. My ultra-short black leather skirt was more akin to a wide belt. And to complete the ensemble, I sentenced my feet to an evening of harsh labor in towering black stilettos. An Asian version of *Will and Grace* we were, your average straight couple we were not.

Giggling like sugar-high children who'd just come out of a candy shop, Tim and I embraced like long lost lovers. We couldn't stop complimenting each other's snazzy outfits. I couldn't help but notice Tim's grin was wider than a slice of watermelon, a telltale sign that mischief was afoot. With all the subtlety of a marching band, Tim dragged me to a secluded corner of the hotel lobby, far from the prying eyes of his colleagues. With the anticipation of a kid unwrapping a birthday present, he spilled the beans.

Tim: "They've just announced our year-end bonus, and it really sucks."

Kim: "How sucky?"

Tim: "Very."

Kim: "Let's drown your sorrows in drinks."

Tim: "Bingo. Let's drink up the bonus that I've been short changed. I've worked it all out. Let's assume this is a regular bar that we usually go to, and we're paying regular prices."

Kim: "Uh huh."

Tim: "We need to do ten drinks each, so I recover at least half of my bonus."

Kim: "OK. Let's do it."

You can bet your boots on Tim's calculations - he's an accountant, after all. The secret sauce of our smooth-sailing, super-fun friendship is a gung-ho, let's-do-it attitude. We're always game for each other's harebrained schemes - no questions asked.

With a foolproof financial plan tucked in our back pocket like a secret weapon, we flung those ballroom doors open like we were unveiling a new phone model. There I was, parading into the less-than-impressive ballroom in my black heels, that while gorgeous, were plotting the death of my feet. My strut was something right out of a high fashion runway show, minus the unreasonable clothing.

Meanwhile, Tim made his entrance, his head shining brighter than a diamond due to an overzealous application of hair gel. He was swaying down an imaginary red carpet in his blindingly glossy Gucci loafers. Suddenly, the crowd fell silent, all eyes on us. For a second, we felt like we'd gatecrashed the wrong party. We were either ridiculously over-dressed or they were severely under-dressed. I'd say it was a case of the latter.

The scene was reminiscent of an elderly bingo night, a sea of folks in the prime of their late 40s or above. They had clearly torn up the rule book on Christmas dressing. While we dressed up, they dressed down. I'm talking fashion choices that would make a thrift store mannequin cringe. Decades-out-of-date floppy cardigans, scruffy shirts under sweaters, baggy pants and skirts with hemlines that plunged many inches below the knees.

If the fashion bar was that low, it was time to hit the bar. There was no second to spare, we had a bonus of 20 drinks to gulp down. The night wasn't young, and neither was this crowd.

We made progress fast. After three drinks each on empty stomachs, we were feeling as light as a couple of helium balloons. We made a mad dash for the budget-friendly, but surprisingly edible, catered food that was doing its best to look fancy at the sides of the ballroom. In between wolfing down canapés and guzzling our fourth drink, we kept up our appearance as a straight couple for Tim's colleagues. "Oh, are you Tim's girlfriend?" they'd ask. I'd nod so hard. It was as if Tim's flamboyant wardrobe hadn't already given us away. Onwards we marched to our fifth, sixth, seventh drink. The more we drank, the more interesting Tim's workmates became. Alcohol is a social lubricant after all.

"Kimmie, meet my boss Vic." My first encounter with Vic was certainly memorable. As Tim's boss and confidante, Vic was the only one in the office Tim trusted enough to come out to. Now, Vic wasn't your typical buttoned-up boss type. Liberal in his thoughts and in his 40s, Vic was a bit of a maverick. His crowning glory? A head full of wild, untamed hair. In their conservative company, men with long hair were as scandalous as being gay. Even today, long after Vic's hung up his corporate boots, him and Tim are still thick as thieves.

Tim let Vic in on our devious plan and he became our personal booze accountant when our math skills drowned in alcohol. By the time we guzzled down our tenth round, our heads were spinning. Our attempt at playing it straight went down the drain once the alcohol took the wheel. Tim? He unleashed his flamboyant dance moves, shredding his "straight guy" cover to confetti on the dance floor.

The following morning, we ruefully admitted, over a

colossal hangover that we had failed miserably at keeping up appearances. We did however smash our ambitious target of 20 drinks. So, was it worth the pounding headache? Yes. Would we do it again? Of course. The years Tim missed his bonus, he'd set a new drink target. We never missed a single target, however prodigious the number. Did he finally come out of his closet? Yes. Surprisingly, Tim wasn't the only gay in the village.

Our annual year-end bash was a tradition as sturdy as our conviction that socks and sandals were a fashion faux pas. From fashion outlaws, we became accepted as fashion forward style icons.

We rolled out the red carpet for fun times, with Vic being our faithful afterparty sidekick. Until one fateful night, when Vic stuck his hand down my underwear. After a few too many cocktails, he'd apparently misplaced his personal boundary map. I didn't know how to broach the subject with Tim. And when I did, Tim didn't know how to broach the subject with Vic. And when he did, Vic apologized. He blamed his cocktail goggles and sensory overload. Needless to say, I've not seen Vic since - there are some lines you just don't cross, and my underwear is one of them.

33

Music Matteo

New York is the mecca of music, bar none. The city boasts some of the most esteemed and legendary music scenes such as the Mercury Lounge, Knitting Factory, Tonic, and Nick's Jazz pub – places I used to frequent. Other notable venues include The Bowery Ballroom, Carnegie Hall, Irving Plaza, Webster Hall, and countless more. It also hosts the prestigious Julliard School of Music, a school for budding young musicians.

Choosing to advance your musical career in the Big Apple is a sound decision. If you're a native, my aren't you the lucky one? Musical geniuses and transplants from across the country or world make their way there to write their stories of success. Some literally end up as music to your ears.

Raised on mainstream tunes, my sonic sensibilities were revolutionized when I moved to New York. The vibrant city was more than a change of scenery; it was a symphony of new sounds that shattered my preconceptions of music. My first purchase in the city was Hope Sandoval's Bavarian Fruit Bread from the legendary Bleecker Street Records, nestled in the Bohemian heart of West Village, a cultural haven now unfortunately closed.

The day I bought that CD is forever etched in my memory, not just for the music, but for the company. Brushing shoulders with Sean Lennon, son of the legendary John Lennon, as he sifted through vinyls remains indelibly imprinted in my memory. It was within the hallowed walls of this record shop that the realms of alternative rock, indie, synth-pop, folk, and post-punk revival unfurled before me like an unexpected pop-up book.

I once dated an award-winning music producer who co-owned an expansive studio in a serene Brooklyn neighborhood with his partner. The studio could easily be mistaken for a secretive music cult's lair. The playroom adjoining the recording studio was a veritable Aladdin's cave, filled to the brim with musical instruments. My earlier stint at a symphony helped me gauge the enormity of their collection, which rivaled the combined total of our wind and brass instruments. The two highly accomplished musicians regularly held uninterrupted music sessions with fellow artists to bash out fresh, thrilling material.

A trailblazer who truly owned and shone at his craft, he played a mad array of musical instruments with effortless coolness and captivating charisma. He knocked things out of the park and produced music for future stars before they had even made their mark. I thank my lucky stars for sighting one such star in the studio before she gained mainstream success.

Securing a front-row seat at a live concert is a prized possession, but having a front-row view to the creation of a musical masterpiece? Priceless. I found myself leagues away from his caliber. Even as a classically-trained pianist, my role was confined to the sidelines, unable to contribute to the explosive creative process. Dwarfed by his towering accomplishments, I had the heebie-jeebies and subsequently bowed out.

The gang partied hard on weekends but made sure to respect the sanctity of Mondays, which marked the beginning of our recovery week. However, to chase away unemployment blues, and in hot pursuit of distractions, I extended my party weekends to include Mondays.

The newest addition to my list had been the Tribeca Grand Hotel, now known as the Roxy Hotel Tribeca. It was famed for throwing the most bustling and hottest Monday media parties in town. Tribeca had become my new playground as I had ventured beyond the pearly gates of glamorous SoHo. I was won over not just by the quiet, low-key charm of the cobbled-stoned Tribeca neighborhood, but also by the convenience of the Tribeca Grand Hotel. It turned out to be a mere ten-minute walk from my SoHo loft. Perfect.

The Tribeca Grand Hotel was more than just a pleasing aesthetic experience. With its sleek, sultry interior design, it exuded an irresistible aura of exclusivity. But beyond its physical allure, the hotel served as a glitzy hotbed for indie films, all thanks to Robert De Niro's annual Tribeca Festival. Once, I nearly got star-struck - literally - when De Niro himself and other stars floated in for the event.

The neighborhood earned the moniker of the "Robert De Niro's patch." Beyond the camera, De Niro led a quiet, unassuming life in his Tribeca loft, embracing the tranquility of this corner of the city. He wasn't just a master of his on-screen roles. He also played a key part in dusting off and transforming this insular part of downtown Manhattan into its prime and flourishing present, where the glitterati are often spotted. De Niro? Still as elusive as ever.

So there I was, cutting a rug at the Tribeca Grand's Monday media bash, when I bumped into Matteo. He tried to work his charm on me, but let's be honest, his flirt game was as coordinated as his two left feet. I kindly friendzoned him on the spot, but he was as relentless as an online pop-up ad. So I thought, why not add this hilarious oddball to my modest gaggle of straight male buddies, mostly made up of former ad agency comrades?

A Music Producer at MTV, Matteo was like the human version of Google Maps for the New York music scene. When the corporate leash was finally taken off at the end of the day, he'd turn into a rockstar, strumming his guitar and belting out tunes with his band.

He whisked me straight into the core of Big Apple's indie scene. We'd hop from one cool kid hangout to another - Tribeca Grand here, Mercury Lounge there. Mercury Lounge, though, was more than just a hangout. It was our indie music temple. This utilitarian, compact and no frills little spot was an unexpected launchpad for some of the best indie artists on the planet.

Mercury Lounge is still standing strong today. Aspiring musicians don't just walk into this place. Oh no, they get down on their knees and pray for a gig here. It's like a rite of passage, a musical baptism if you will. I mean, just look at the roll call. Radiohead, The Yeah Yeah Yeahs, Interpol and Arcade Fire, all of them cut their teeth here. And let's not forget the divas. Lady Gaga, Katy Perry, Lana Del Ray, they all belted out their tunes in this very place before the world knew their names.

We saw The Killers rock the stage here in 2004. In 2005, they snagged the *MTV Music Video Award* for *Best New Artist* and was named the *World's Best Selling New Group* at the *World Music Awards*. Their album *Hot Fuzz* was certainly hot stuff, having earned three *Grammy Awards* nominations.

If I had a nickel for every musical score Matteo and I discovered together. Matteo was like my personal musical tour guide, introducing me to scenes I didn't even know existed. We dove into the underbelly of Alphabet City, finding hidden treasure troves of musical genius in dive bars that weren't even blips on the average person's radar.

Tonic, Mercury Lounge, Tribeca Grand, you name it, we were there. Music never slept. Neither did we. Even when the last stragglers were kicked out of the venues, we didn't stop. Oh no, we just moved the party to my place, swapping state-of-the-art speakers for my budget home sound system.

Nestled in a symphony of music with Matteo, I didn't have a care in the world about visas, jobs, boyfriends or the other pesky New York nuisances that gnawed at my sanity. Lo and behold, a month later, I landed a gig at another agency.

It handed me my golden visa and a paycheck. Nothing more. Deep down, I felt that there was a whole ocean of creativity in the Big Apple I had yet to dive into. Agency work was just a pit stop, a stepping stone.

Matteo had always carried a torch for me. He had harbored hopes that I would change my mind and begin to see him as more than a friend, as a romantic interest. To me, he was my kindred spirit in music.

One evening at a dingy dive bar, he made a last-ditch attempt to turn our friendship into something more. My heart declined his offer, causing him pain despite my best efforts to soften the blow. But unlike before, he didn't persist. Instead, he chose silence, sounding the end of our friendship. I was cut deep.

As I sit here, the past twenty years seem to blur into a montage of joy, music, and at times, heartbreak. It's a story that's been buried deep within me, waiting for the right moment to surface. He was the catalyst that sparked my passion for indie music, a passion that would define me in ways I could never have imagined. He deserves more than a passing mention in this book. He deserves a chapter of his own, a tribute to the profound influence he had on me.

34

Checkmate

Approaching men has never been my forte. I've always been drawn to the type of man who isn't afraid to be bold, to step up and take charge. Call me old-fashioned, but to me, this is what defines a man's strength and character. The only exception was Nasser, a Lebanese American I encountered at a humble dive bar in the Alphabet City.

Let me set the scene of the encounter. It was eight at night, and I found myself nestled in the center of a decrepit, elongated wooden bar counter. I cautiously placed my Southern Comfort and Sprite down on a shabby paper coaster, my gaze wandering over the countertop, a canvas marred by more inscriptions than an ancient tablet. Poetry, professions of love, and cryptic phone numbers, all scribbled and carved over the years, were now etched into an endless tableau of time.

In the dim and narrow tavern, red neon lights radiated a sultry glow. A few locals, mostly in search of cheap beer and greasy grub on a weekday, populated the place. The seating was precariously held together with duct tape, hinting at the bar's rugged charm. Band posters from the past, faded and vandalized, were haphazardly stuck to the walls. These quintessential characteristics are what defined dive bars.

I glanced to my right and spotted a young Middle-Eastern man, rocking a crisp white tee and sky-blue jeans. He was deep in a chess book, so engrossed he didn't even notice the ear-splitting Indie-punk music screeching from the budget speakers. The book? 'Kasparov Teaches Chess' - a vintage paperback with brown pages and a cover that's seen better days. His beer glass was half-full, or half-empty depending on your life philosophies, and had been ignored so long the coaster was starting to look like a mini waterbed.

Stunned at finding a Kasparov reader in a bar, I couldn't resist approaching him. After all, dive bars are social hubs. Downing my Southern Comfort for courage, I made my first ever move on a man - a pawn move in the game of chess.

"Hey. That's a pretty wild choice of book you've got there" I blurted out, trying to hide my jitters. Nasser didn't even blink. The words 'Abort! Abort! Abort!' ran laps in my mind. I chewed my lip like it was bubblegum. He shot me a quick, 'Are-you-talking-to-me?' glance, then held up a finger, like a librarian asking for quiet. After finishing the mother of all sentences, he finally put his bookmark to use and closed the book. "Hello. It's a mesmerizing read," Nasser replied, finally acknowledging my existence.

Nasser seemed as bashful as a schoolboy with a secret crush. After my near-disastrous icebreaker, I was at a loss on planning my next move. It felt like I'd barged into his blissful book bubble. "A Kasparov in a noisy dive bar? That's very impressive," I complimented him. He chuckled and bashfully did the classic look-down-and-blush move. "Just dipping my toes into the chess world. Thought I'd swot up on some strategies from the book."

With a little effort, I managed to coax a conversation out of him. Turns out, he's a freshly minted master's graduate from Cornell University. Born and bred in the city with Lebanese roots, courtesy of his parents. The more we jawed, the more his bashful, soft-spoken charm grew on me. Then in strolled Matteo and I placed my business card on his Kasparov book, a symbolic gesture that the next move was on him. "Call me some time," I said, all cool and collected, while my insides twisted into nervous knots.

Weeks went by on a blur. I was prancing around the town with Matteo, hitting up every joint from the Mercury

Lounge to the Tribeca Grand. My first romantic fumble had slipped my mind. Then Matteo ghosted me. Suddenly, I was staring down a huge hole in my social life.

Out of the digital blue, a friendly text popped onto my screen. It was Nasser, suddenly feeling the urge to apologize for his radio silence. You'd think he was a cat trying to play it cool after falling off a shelf. Then came the redemption, swift and sweet. He claimed my business card had been moonlighting as his bookmark, meaning every time he cracked open a book, there I was. For all his bookish smarts, I suspected that when it came to the love department, he might be as smooth as sandpaper.

Nasser scored an invite from his cousin to a Johnnie Walker tasting event and casually asked if I fancied being his plus one. My insides were once again turning but I had to play it cool. Now, according to barstool wisdom, a little liquid courage tends to coax our innermost sentiments out into the open. Johnnie Walker might just be the magic potion to help Nasser pole-vault right over his bashfulness.

So, the big date night finally rolled around. I spotted Nasser outside the swanky watering hole where the evening's spirits tasting was set to take place. We exchanged the customary cheek-to-cheek kisses, and I must say, he had taken the dress code up a few notches. From denim casual in a dive bar, he had upgraded to snazzy black button-down and dress pants, fit for a swanky bar. I was all set to snuggle into the night with him when he dropped the cousin bomb. Apparently, we were expecting a third wheel - his cousin. It was Ziad who had scored the tasting invites.

Upon entering, we were wowed by the gorgeous bar, clearly designed for style lovers looking to imbibe. The bar, usually serving up stirred cocktails, had been reserved exclusively for a high-society tasting event. We were escorted to our seating arrangement, a curved plush sofa, where a table was already set for three. Atop the table sat elegant and expertly polished Glencairn glasses, their simple yet sophisticated design catching the soft lighting of the room. Alongside the glasses, a glass water carafe stood tall at the height of style on the table. This carafe, filled to the brim, served as an assuring promise to pace our evening.

The bar swiftly brimmed with guests. Sensing my unease, Nasser assured me that his cousin was his lifeline in moments of verbal drought.

"Seat's taken?" Suddenly, a head popped up between Nasser and me, nearly making us jump out of our skins. Nasser, rolling his eyes so hard I thought they might fall out, begrudgingly introduced the new intruder. With a cheeky grin, Ziad wedged himself next to me, completely ignoring the vacant throne next to Nasser. We had to shimmy our lovely derrières to the right, to make room for Ziad's unorthodox seating arrangement. Nasser let out a dramatic sigh and gave Ziad a look that could curdle milk.

"You must be Kim." Ziad flashed a grin and offered me his hand. I shook it, momentarily hypnotized by his emerald eyes, twinkling like a pair of mischievous leprechauns. His blonde hair was a symphony of waves, blonde surfers riding the tanned skin of his forehead. The guy was a walking, talking romance novel cover - tall, broad, and exotic.

I couldn't fathom how Nasser and Ziad were related. Ziad, sensing my confusion, clarified, "I'm half German, half Lebanese, and yes, we're cousins." They were as different as chalk and cheese. Ziad could talk faster than a used car salesman and was so funny you'd risk a hernia from laughing. The evening progressed from a taste test to an AB test of who I was to end up with.

The whisky sommelier kicked off the evening when guests settled into their seats. We went through the motions of sniffing aromatics and picking up subtle notes of the whisky. Then took small careful sips, did the roll back, felt the top notes and ethanol burn down our throats.

In the grand tradition of whisky amateurs, we opted to go for sizeable amounts of whisky as the night progressed. Ziad, the certified charmer, had my attention in a vice grip, flirting like it was his day job. Meanwhile, our sommelier and Nasser were practically invisible. Nasser quietly burnt with rage at the side, as more ethanol burnt down our throats.

As the night turned fuzzy, guests turned into cocktail revelers post tasting session. Ziad played bartender, and Nasser knocked back fast, which knocked him out fast. Soon enough he was out cold, folded over like a lawn chair. Ziad was practically glued to my side. One had to put up quite a struggle to resist a cover star of romance novels. I managed to make my great escape, darting off to the all-gender restroom downstairs like a fugitive seeking refuge.

As I was exiting my stall, Ziad, acting like the protagonist in a romance novel, swooped his muscular arms around me. He gently forced me back into the stall and drove his tongue inside my mouth. Then he released my mouth and whispered seductively, "you are mine". He secured the door, firmly grasped my hair with one hand and held my bottom with the other. I gazed into his captivating green eyes, now filled with desire, and plastered my mouth on his. At that moment, I desired him. He was everything that Nasser wasn't. As he skillfully unhooked my bra and pressed his aroused body against mine, Nasser began pounding on the door. He hollered, "Hey, what are you guys doing? I want in!"

Drawing away from the heated kiss with Ziad, my gaze fell on his incredibly green eyes. The fervor between us slowly simmered down, and Ziad replied with a resigned tone, "Nothing much. We're coming out!"

Bursting out of the stall, our faces were flushed with fiery passion and my hair was in a wild tumble. Nasser suggested we go to my place for drinks, his legs shaky from intoxication. I had nearly finished AB testing, leaning towards one hypothesis, but the evening's outcome was uncertain. Despite initial hesitation, I agreed to host, emboldened by the alcohol.

Upon reaching my place, we indulged in another round of drinks, lounging casually on the sofa. Suddenly, Ziad leaned in, capturing my lips with a burning intensity. I resisted momentarily, acutely aware of Nasser's watchful gaze, before succumbing to the intoxicating fervor of his kiss. Anchoring myself on his robust arms, I felt the strength radiating from him. He paused momentarily to discard his shirt and pants, his boxers following suit, revealing his sculpted muscular legs. Throughout, his hypnotic green eyes never strayed from mine. In a stroke, he leaned in, positioning himself between my legs.

"May I join?" Nasser interjected, stark naked, his arousal more primal than sensual. Amidst our escalating passion, Ziad and I hadn't noticed him disrobing.

My gaze flickered between Ziad and Nasser, both ready for hot action. I was caught in a sexual dilemma, sandwiched between two men. It was no longer a choice of one or the other, but of a pair or a trio - an uncharted territory for me. Simply put, the AB test had evolved into an ABC test.

Despite my deep longing for Ziad, I forced myself to reject him. The idea of a risqué ménage à trois nauseated me. Yes, this was New York City, and undoubtedly, thousands of such encounters were probably happening that very night. Thousands of passionate moans released. Thousands of 69 plus one's. Thousands of intimate, three-way spooning's. Yet, I couldn't bring myself to partake.

"I need both of you to leave," I firmly demanded. The cousins, wide-eyed, froze like a scene from a life-drawing class. I pointed at the door to emphasize my point. Finally understanding my seriousness, they hurriedly dressed. Ziad tried a final romantic gesture, pulling me close and pleading with his smoldering green eyes. Despite the move being straight out of a romance novel, I stayed firm, shook my head, and guided them towards the exit.

The last time I saw Nasser was at that early morning soiree. I silently wished his chess skills surpassed his knack for love strategy. By inviting Ziad into our equation, he inadvertently checkmated himself. As I penned this chapter, curiosity led me to dig into his whereabouts. I was delighted to discover that he had ascended to a much-coveted Chief position. It seems his strategic prowess finds a better playground on the corporate chessboard.

Note to self - do not make the first move on men. This lesson has been deeply ingrained. When they are given the chance to take the lead, you give them an opportunity to reveal their true nature.

As for threesomes, it's still not my cuppa. I have come a long way in my sexual odyssey and threesomes simply don't fit into it. Ethical sluts, kinky feminists and liberalists may label me a prude, but I perceive threesomes as crude. A single, authentic connection still holds a special charm for me.

35

Belarussian Roulette

I was wrapped up in Soviet history and literature, but I hadn't wrapped my legs around anyone from the former Soviet Union. I perceived them to be preferentially endogamous, and the cultural chasm between us would be too vast for a relationship to succeed.

My world view was put to the test when I encountered Andrei from Belarus on Craigslist. As I anxiously awaited the approval of my second H-1B visa, I diverted my attention with the pursuit of romance. Andrei, in his Craigslist advertisement, portrayed himself as an immigrant from Belarus with a profound love for arts and culture. This made him stand out from the crowd.

When we met in person, Andrei, a thin, pale figure in his early 30s, immediately tickled my funny bone. His boyish charm, amplified by his large, inquisitive brown eyes and a Russian accent thicker than a Siberian winter, was unexpectedly captivating. Not my usual cup of tea, but his seamless transition from clownish to intense had a magnetic pull on me.

Being the only son of a single mother, he left Belarus, a landlocked country, as a teenager, before it achieved independence in 1991. He was born into hardship, grew up amidst it, and became thoroughly familiar with it. Like most first-generation immigrants, he faced struggles in the land of the free.

Living in a foreign country often thrusts us into a whirlpool of struggles. We lug along our ingrained set of culture, but to blend in, adaptation is unavoidable. This cultural collision can trigger an intense identity crisis, leaving us questioning – how much authenticity can I maintain? How much of myself should I conceal? Immersing in a new environment can be exhilarating yet disheartening, as feelings of alienation creep in.

Having secured a place at a high school, Andrei was filled with hopes of a fresh start and a new circle of friends. However, after the highs came the lows; he was isolated, bullied, and made to feel like an utter outcast.

Could I identify with this? My tenure at two separate agencies in New York left me feeling like an outsider. I am neither American, white, nor male, and I always felt inadequate. Ironically, at the second agency I worked for, there were two unpleasant Singaporeans who showed prejudice towards me simply because I hadn't resided in the US for as long as they had. They had endured their own struggles and discrimination upon arriving in New York and decided to impose this initiation on me without my consent. Adding to my sense of alienation and discomfort.

There's also the need to succeed. The drive to excel intensifies when you've escaped severe economic or political conditions in your native land. You didn't uproot your life just to be insignificant in your new home. Living in a dynamic city like the Big Apple cranks up the pressure valve even more. The mantra 'Go big or go home' rings even more true.

The inspiration to pen this book came from those who didn't succeed, as per societal or personal definitions. A lot of us slipped through the cracks, we are the unsung heroes who dared to take on the formidable challenges of the Big Apple. Whenever we stumbled, we picked ourselves up, dusted off and carried on. The realities we encountered were a far cry from our dreams, but we soldiered on, trying to make sense of it all.

My Big Apple story wasn't one of success but one of survival. Having a home in my native country to retreat to, I can now view my entire experience as a grand adventure, marking a significant chapter in my life. I'm aware of many who were, and remain, trapped in the Big Apple.

Right from the beginning, Andrei and I had a few common denominators which made us a good equation. Being culturally adaptable and having a curiosity for different cultures, I found myself drawn towards his Russian heritage. Our second date was at the famed Pravda, a Russian-themed SoHo speakeasy and cocktail lounge, hidden away in the dark basement of Lafayette. Before it was forced to close down like many of its nightlife counterparts, it was a hotspot for Russian natives who swore by all 21 varietals of their vodkas and authentic Russian bites. New York celebs and SoHo types couldn't agree more.

Andrei cranked up our Russian immersion in Brighton Beach, the 'Little Odessa' of New York. This charming, sleepy town, brimming with Soviet Union immigrants, feels like a mini Russia. Here, you'll hear Russian and Ukrainian more than English, and see Cyrillic signs everywhere. Shops are stocked with Russian goodies, and it's practically a crime to leave without some caviar and vodka. And remember when CDs and DVDs were all the rage? Well, this place was like the Hollywood of Russian entertainment.

Food is our delicious hotline to our culture and identity. I mean, who can resist the comforting call of a home-cooked meal? Andrei and his mom had their own gastronomic pilgrimage in Brighton Beach every week and I was the lucky third wheel. My taste buds did a Russian folk dance with stroganoff, pelmeni, borscht, and blini. Even started guzzling vodka during lunch. It was one wild, yummy cultural adventure, and I loved every slurp and sip.

Andrei, a wizard in the kitchen, started serving up Russian feasts at home, taking turns with his roomie, Eloi. Just like that, I became a regular patron of the Belarussian Supper Club.

When it came to Andrei, there was just one little fly in my chardonnay - his address. He was shacked up in a roomy pad in Harlem with his buddies and workmates Eloi and Viktor. Remember my neighborhood no-go list? Harlem was on it. But for Andrei, I made an exception. It was miles away from the downtown hustle, and light-years from SoHo's shining sophistication.

The Belarussian Super Club had additional members like Eloi's Russian sweetheart and Viktor's American girlfriend. I couldn't stand Viktor from the get-go. A rabid talker and rabble rouser, he had a vile temper, accompanied by very archaic views of women. A controversial opinion of his was that a woman's place was in the kitchen, existing solely to cater to the whims of men. Talk about living in the Stone Age. According to him, women were supposed to be seen and not heard. I kid you not. Every time he started spewing his caveman philosophies, I felt like I was choking on a prehistoric bone. Everyone kept silent, for fear of unleashing more of his wrath.

You might be curious about his girlfriend. A tale befitting a soap opera indeed, but I'll keep it brief. Viktor, a dashing blonde alpha-male, initially charmed everyone as a Prince Charming. But soon, he unveiled his true colors, morphing into a Prince Alarming instead.

When I first met his girlfriend, I had to do a reality pinch test. Natalia was severely obese, pale, cross-eyed and bespectacled. Her appearance suggested that she suffered from severe low self-esteem. The gap age between the Natalia and Viktor was a gulf. She was merely 20 while Viktor was in his early 30s. Fearfully hiding in Viktor's shadows, she struggled to speak most times. On the few occasions she did, Viktor would throw shade at her.

Alright, just to get this straight before you accuse me of body-shaming, there was absolutely nothing wrong with how she looked. It was their pairing up that caused a couple of eyebrows to hitch a ride north - it was one of those Transformers-type situations, more than meets the eye.

After a few rounds of my KGB-styled interrogations, Andrei folded like a cheap suit. He let slip that Natalia's grandpa, who was rolling in dough, had recently kicked the bucket. A mountain of money was coming her way, but there was a catch - she had to wait until she hit the big 2-1. Meanwhile, Viktor was like an eagle scout, keeping his eyes on the cookie jar. That was all Andrei was willing to reveal. And honestly, it was enough to put two and two together.

The dynamics got weirder in the Belarussian Supper Club. Viktor began publicly berating Natalia to the point that she wept buckets. As Andrei swore me to secrecy about Viktor's evil ploy, there was little comfort I could provide to Natalia. She was younger, naive and too different from me. All I wanted was a free pass to skip the Belarusian Supper Club, whenever Viktor and Natalia decided to turn up.

The trio ran a collectibles business on eBay. They were so tight-knit you'd think they were born glued together. Their idea of a social life was like an exclusive club, with a membership of exactly three. Now, Andrei, he was the ringleader and the most sensible, keeping everything under control and the other two out of trouble. They ran a very tight-lipped operation, and even though I was practically furniture in their home, I was just a bystander. Not that I minded, I wasn't exactly jumping at the bit to join their little eBay brigade, anyway.

One day, Andrei popped the question - not the marriage one, the cohabitation one. Now, as much as I liked him, giving up my chic SoHo digs and my high-gloss lifestyle for his Russian frat house? No thank you.

But then, destiny hit the gas pedal and a spot opened up in the unit below Andrei's. He promptly banished Eloi and Viktor downstairs. I decided to make a mini move. I started salt-and-peppering the place with some of my essentials and a couple of my statement outfits. Yet, I confidently held onto my SoHo haven for my daytime adventures. And oh boy, was I glad that I did.

SoHo to Harlem was a quantum leap from one planet to another. In SoHo, I felt free, spirited and uplifted. I flitted from store to store, bar to bar, café to café, eatery to eatery, with a high five with staff and owners turned friends at every landing. In Harlem, I felt like I was flirting with death. Always on high alert, with a constant fear of attack.

In Harlem then, the hottest new trend was the Subway

Shove, where folks were nudged onto a platform just as a train was barreling in. Apparently, this still persists in some city corners. My survival strategy? Stand as far from the platform as possible, and only sprint for the train when it came to a full stop. It was like a daily episode of "Survivor: Subway Edition."

In the neighborhood, it was so wild that even the fast food joints had bulletproof glass. I thought I was ordering a burger, not robbing a bank. Andrei had to explain to me that it wasn't a local delicacy. It was a mystery to me how a place for quick bites became a place for quick bucks.

A string of Bodega robberies rocked the neighborhood. One fine day, I'd just hopped off the subway in Harlem, catching my breath and patting myself on the back for yet another successful, near-death-experience-free commute. As I emerged from the underground, I caught sight of a NY1 news van, parked up and looking all official. The back doors coyly ajar like a flirtatious wink, revealing a reporter having a last-minute nose powder, prepping for his on-air moment.

Cordoned off from the public was my local store, now a hive of police activity. And there, smack dab in front of me, was a chalk outline on the pavement. Seems they'd just carted off a 'dearly departed'. A legit crime scene, right there in front of me, and I did a little jig of terror. A day in the life, just a day in the life.

Doing laundry in SoHo was a breeze. I'd chill with a book. In Harlem, it was like a high-stakes game, keeping an eagle eye on my laundry. With the Belarussian warnings of laundry theft, I felt like a laundry detective.

Strolling through Harlem became less of a leisurely walk and more of an adventure into the wild unknown. Quite the contrast from the laid-back vibe of SoHo, where the only danger is tripping over a rogue cobblestone.

It wasn't all gloom in Harlem. It had its perks, namely the lip-smacking soul food from Sylvia's Restaurant and the toe-tapping tunes at St. Nick's Jazz pub. This joint was so famous, even the busloads of tourists knew to swing by for some top-quality jazz. Night after night, the musicians would blow their hearts and lungs out, turning the audiences into wild, jazz-crazed maniacs. Alas, the jazz pub has now pulled down its shutters, joining the list of legendary closed shops mentioned in this book.

Friends were instructed not to surprise me in Harlem, where I was always on high alert with my trusty pepper spray. Sud made light of the situation by joking about needing passports for a trip to Harlem, while Tim mournfully noted they'd "lost a friend" to the neighborhood.

I was a fish out of water, plopped into a frozen pond of Belarussians who could out-ice an ice cube. Stuck between being true to myself and trying to fit into this frosty world, my only lifeline was Andrei. He was my cheerleader, my salesperson, convincing me daily to stick it out. I needed a break, some space to think. And in a turn of events as predictable as a sitcom, the universe heard me and delivered.

The business trio began frequenting LA. Andrei mentioned business expansion, but details? Not my thing. Each time he left, I'd bolt for my SoHo loft, finding clarity in his absence. One night, pre-flight, Andrei sat me down for a heart to heart chat.

Andrei: "Listen, baby. I have been meaning to tell you something."

Me: "What is it?"

Andrei: "We don't run an eBay business."

Andrei paused, eyeballing my reaction before continuing.

Andrei: "We run three online porn businesses."

He paused again, after dropping that bombshell on me.

Me: "Three online porn businesses?"

Andrei: "Yes. One's for golden showers, another for spanking, and the last for all types of porn."

How I wish I could serve this story to you as it was served to me - cushioned in a thick, fluffy blanket of Russian accent. The scene was part stand-up comedy, part Twilight Zone. Now, Andrei had a pet word - 'thrash'. While most of us would zip through that in a single syllable, he'd break it into a two-part series and give that 'r' a good roll. It would come out sounding like 'te-rrrrrrash'

Me: "Te-rrrrrash business?"

Andrei chuckled and agreed, clearly amused by my joke.

Me: "Why are you telling me this now?"

Andrei: "We've decided to get into porn productions. We usually buy the content. Now, we'll make them."

It was a nuclear bomb, camouflaged as, well, a bomb. Oh. My. Lord. Was there no end to the confession?

Andrei: "We'll run two production houses. One here and one in L.A."

I kept my silence, and he delivered the final denouement.

Andrei: "We'll be doing casting calls here in the apartment, and you'll be seeing some weird things happening."

No shit, Sherlock.

Andrei: "I get that you need time to deal with this. I'm aware you're unhappy here. I deeply regret lying. Fear of rejection kept me from being honest. I can't lie anymore. I'll return in a week, hoping we're still together. I love you dearly."

I had a lump at the back of my throat. To be clear, the lump was the chunk of unexpected news shoved down my throat. As I deciphered his message, I eventually dropped this bombshell on the equally shocked gang.

In the aftermath, I retreated to my technicolor SoHo sanctuary. There, I toyed with a startling idea - becoming the Spielberg of the skin flicks industry. Not in front of the camera, mind you. I'm not one for getting frisky in front of a lens, the world isn't ready for my naked glory. No, I fantasized about being the genius behind the raunchiest scripts ever written. But eventually, I te-rrrrashed those thoughts like a bad tabloid headline.

Let's be real, this wasn't a bunny burrow I wanted to hop into. I've got my own band of misfits and our little bubble that I could easily boomerang back to. Staking your claim in the world is like setting your name in wet cement - it's all about accepting your quirky self and feeling like you belong. This is even more important when you're in a foreign land, where you're probably wondering if you fit in and trying to get your bearings.

When you do eventually stumble upon your

community and tribe, it's like finding the missing puzzle piece to your identity. You're accepted, embraced, celebrated and before you know it, you're building friendships and relationships, and your self-worth shoots up faster than a rocket. I totally got that he needed to be accepted for who he was, like a bird needs to fly. But I couldn't accept him for his job - I mean, he belonged to his world, and I belonged to mine, like two pieces of a jigsaw puzzle that just didn't fit.

Andrei didn't bug me, aware that I needed space to process their weighty secret he guarded so well. Three days later, I vacated Harlem forever, leaving behind only a heartfelt farewell letter for Andrei. It ended with, "I love you very much too." I never glanced back; that was never my style.

36

An Act of Love

Single and looking for love in the Big Apple? Navigating through this labyrinth of potential love can feel like hunting for a needle in a haystack. The Big Apple, in matters of the heart, emerges as an alluring yet elusive fruit in the Garden of Eden. Dare to yield to its intoxicating allure and brace yourself for a potential paradise lost. I have borne witness to the poignant descent of many who gave in to this irresistible temptation, their regret evident as it washed over them.

Conversely, the Big Apple also presents itself as an enticing apple of passion, ripe and beckoning you to have a succulent bite. After that, nothing substantial occurs, you simply relish your chomps.

The singletons in the gang would often bemoan the trials and tribulations of city dating. We'd gather every Sunday, nursing our brunch-time Bloody Marys and trading tales more terrifying than a horror flick. We've wooed weirdos, dated the commitment-phobic, and even tangoed with a few genuine crazies. For ages, the city that never sleeps earned a new title: the city that never loves. This was one of our greatest fears, perhaps an unfounded one.

Tim and Simon have been a duo for 20 years, with Sud hitched and a surrogate parent. After Thaddeus, Vinny found love and has been happy for years. Claire left NYC, found love elsewhere. My story? That's another book. Let's stick to this one first.

Just like Adam and Eve, you've got choices. Dating is an apple-sorting bonanza. You're after the golden delicious, not the rotten Granny Smith. But beware, some apples are Oscar-worthy actors, all shiny on the outside but a letdown once you sink your teeth in. It's a fruit salad of chance, so brace yourself and take that first bite.

I met Jude at a bar in Brooklyn while visiting Jai. Jai had managed to scrape together enough pennies to nab himself a dreamy little pad in a much-coveted, classic and rare brownstone in Williamsburg. More than a beautiful townhouse, a historical brownstone is a shining status symbol. You could say I was bursting with pride for Jai, planting his roots in the big city and all. Though I did shed a tear or two when he ditched SoHo.

Well, we may have split up, but you'd be surprised how

much toilet paper can keep two lives intertwined. We spent years together, as partners in crime, then as partners in prime real estate in SoHo. He was my go-to guy, my rock, my midnight snack buddy. He was just a stone's throw away from my loft, which was super convenient when I ran out of snacks. Or toilet paper. I lost not only my SoHo mate but also my toilet paper supplier. It felt like the final flush of our relationship - he had moved out and moved on.

Brooklyn, the cool cousin amongst NYC's five boroughs, is a laidback, spacious, and family-friendly retreat from Manhattan's frenzied city life. It's also wallet-friendly until you hit gentrified Williamsburg where property prices have skyrocketed.

On my free-spirited Brooklyn weekend trips, I'd visit Jai. Suddenly, I found myself with time on my hands, having finally broken free from the chains of a visa-bound, mediocre sweatshop disguised as an agency. I initially beamed with pride at landing a top agency job in NYC, but desperation led me to a second one for salary and visa. As a creative who took great pride in my work, I was conditioned to work on prolific brands, crack tough briefs, deliver top-notch, original, and measurable creative campaigns, and chase awards.

At the second agency, I was teamed with a spirit-crushing and mercurial bitch-from-hell Art Director from Singapore. The Creative Director struggled to pair Cruella with American Copywriters, all of whom quit. Perhaps he thought a visa and shared nationality would convince me to stick around.

Why did they keep her on staff? Well, she was like a human vacuum cleaner, sucking up all the dull and grimy tasks that everyone else treated like leftover meatloaf. Her social life was as bustling as a ghost town, no friends in sight, not even a long-lost cousin in the US or Singapore. She swapped one lion's den in Singapore for another in New York, erecting a ramshackle kingdom of solitude. Not me though, I wasn't about to toss my precious life into the ring. Her presence was like adding a wasp sting to the usual advertising swamp of racism, sexism, and bullying. Finding myself in a corner once more, I decided to throw in my bloody towel.

Whenever life gave me lemons, Jai was there, ready with the tequila. There I was again, at life's favorite fork in the road - to ditch the bright lights of the Big Apple, or not? But first, a little detour - time to visit Jai in his spanking new brownstone in Williamsburg.

After our jolly catch up, I decided to grab a swift solo drink before my train ride. If you really want to get under a neighborhood's skin, you've got to check out its watering holes. So, I went on a little bar safari down Main Street and ended up in this no-frills joint that oozed chill vibes. The bar was full of solo drinkers, but I wasn't in the mood to talk, so I snagged a booth and snuggled up with my Noam Chomsky's 'Understanding Power'. Nothing like a dense political read to lighten up your bar experience.

Ever feel like you're being eyeballed? I sure did, and just like that, my book needed a timeout. I glanced over to the bar and there he was, a Latino heartthrob, in his early 20s, sporting hair as black as midnight and skin as smooth and shiny as an olive in a martini. Dressed in an olive shirt that was two sneezes away from falling off his slender frame, and cargo pants so baggy they'd make MC Hammer envious.

In the lineup of fashion disasters and average Joes, this guy was a unicorn. As I stared, he snuck a cheeky peek my way. "Busted!" I chuckled to myself, shooting him a grin bright enough to power a small city.

Caught red-handed, he just dropped his gaze and smiled, all shy like. Then he swung his legs off his bar stool and sauntered over with the casualness of a cat. His smile vanished, replaced with a serious look, courtesy of his bushy eyebrows. With a swift spin, he teased past me then boomeranged back. His face folded into a warm smile as he plopped down beside me. Up close, his glossy puppy eyes had the power to play puppet master with your heartstrings. My racing heart needed a taming anyway. His eyelashes were so lush, it was like he'd been born with natural mascara.

Through our first convo, I discovered Jude was a Brooklyn-born Puerto Rican, marking a first in my love life adventure. When he dropped the Puerto Rican bomb, my mental encyclopedia was as empty as a politician's promises. I had zero clue about the country and its culture.

Jude was a movie and TV actor, not a notable Tinseltown celebrity. His claim to fame? Scoring a gig in a Latin American movie. A method actor who went to a renowned acting school, he spent his days in auditions or acting out scenes. And here I am in New York, dating a whole United Nations of men.

Jude and I were practically super-glued together, day and night. Only the lure of rehearsals or casting calls could pry him away from my loft. After a traumatizing near-move to Harlem, I put my foot down on a move to Brooklyn.

We'd start chatting at the crack of dawn and wouldn't stop until our eyelids started making deals with gravity. Remember when you found your kindred spirit, and you conversed so smoothly it's like you're doing a verbal ballet? That was us, words pouring out, electrifying the air, giving each other life updates like we're in a speed dating event. When our word well ran dry, we'd just bask in the golden silence, still connected like two phones with a full WiFi signal. Jude, the shy whisperer, and me, the talkative town crier. We were a perfect yin and yang – when he ebbed, I flowed. When I ebbed, he flowed.

New York is like a worldwide buffet, with a smorgasbord of cultures and ethnicities. It's like walking through the United Nations on lunch break. I had a hilarious realization though - I thought I was a fan of Latino food, until someone dropped the bomb that Tex-Mex isn't really Latino or Mexican.

My relationship with Jude opened my eyes to the vibrant culture of Puerto Rico. Puerto Ricans, who arrived in NYC in droves during the 1950s "Great Migration", make up the city's second-largest Hispanic community. They now constitute 8.9 per cent of NYC's population and a significant 32 per cent of its Latino demographic. Their rich heritage is celebrated in the annual Puerto Rican Day Parade, the oldest and longest running Latino parade in the city. I had the privilege of attending this electric event once, and it was nothing short of exhilarating.

I was practically bouncing off the walls with these bite-sized Puerto Rican knowledge nuggets, while Jude felt his American identity was his birthright. It wasn't that he was denying his Latino lineage, he was more Americanized than Puerto Ricanized. Now, as a Singaporean with Chinese blood, if Jude started throwing around facts about my lineage that I didn't resonate with, I'd be as weirded out.

Jude was the epitome of a home-loving Latino, with the habits of a sloth. Once the appeal of lazy mornings started waning, I lured him out from his comfort zone into my eclectic world of museums, art galleries, and movies. Despite his fondness for these, particularly movies, the allure of home always held him captive. Our social gatherings dwindled, but the gang understood - we were in the blissful honeymoon phase of our relationship, happily nested in our love cocoon.

Our contrasting lifestyles began to strain our relationship. I yearned to return to my dynamic life, hoping to involve him. However, he was equally determined to remain immersed in our shared solitude.

Party Central was back in full swing after a long hibernation, and the gang was stoked. Jude, however, played hard to get, initially offering lame excuses before outright confessing he wanted no part in it. But, the real head scratcher was his stubborn demand for a text when our parties were winding down.

Like clockwork, Jude always appeared after the last party guest had stumbled out. Tim and Simon, the self-appointed party wardens, were always baffled by his impeccable timing. He wasn't the wild type, but he sure knew how to handle a post-party cleanup. And then, as the dust settled, he'd curl up next to me in bed, as if we were just a normal couple. He was a peculiar code that Tim, Simon and I couldn't crack.

One dawn, post a crazy party, my frustration erupted like a volcano. Tim and Simon, like seasoned relay athletes, handed the clean-up baton to Jude. Sensing a storm brewing, they conveniently disappeared when Jude took over. While he was elbow-deep in dishes, I demanded to know why he skipped the parties. He clammed up as usual. So, I did what men dread most - I gave him an ultimatum.

The words worked like magic. Jude delicately washed a wine glass with the precision of a surgeon, gave his hands a good scrub, and dried them with a flourish. Then, his hand dove into his pocket for his wallet, and my heart plunged into my stomach. Was he about to pull out a snapshot of a secret wife and kids he'd been hiding?

In a relief-inducing maneuver, he extracted a neatly folded newspaper clipping, its edges yellowed by time, and placed it before me. "What's this?" I inquired, my curiosity piqued. "Read it," he replied, poker-faced. The suspense was killing me. If this was an act, it was the epitome of method acting I'd ever witnessed.

I grappled with including this chapter, hesitant to deviate from what I believed to be accurate. I aimed for authenticity throughout this memoir, not stories of verisimilitudes. In the name of privacy, I altered certain names in the memoir. I had to be cautious not to reveal Jude's identity, given our easy access to information today. Jude, who I recently found out is still in the acting business, deserves his privacy respected. The following details of the news article are altered.

I read the headline aloud, "Man steals endangered bog turtle from the Bronx Zoo". Struggling to comprehend due to either confusion or the effects of alcohol, Jude took over and read the article. I heard phrases like "When he was arrested, he threatened to cook and eat the Bog Turtle", "The Bog turtle was sick and under medication", "He defended his action as an act of love, claiming he could care for it better than the zookeepers." I was caught between laughter and shock, unable to believe such a ludicrous theft. Then Jude made the connection.

Jude: "It was me. I did it."

Me: "What do you mean you did it?"

Jude: "I stole the bog turtle."

Me: "Why would you do that?"

Jude: "It was an act of love. It's written in the article."

Me: "Gimme that."

I delicately seized the article from his grasp, my eyes hungrily devouring each word. Jude's name was woven through the lines, tying him indisputably to the crime. One line stood out: the police had discovered Jude's plan to sell the endangered bog turtle for a hefty sum. This wasn't just news, it was a plot straight out of a low-budget thriller.

Me: "What kind of animal does that?"

Jude: "The kind that steals animals."

The wisecrack nearly cracked me up, but I didn't want to encourage him as I wasn't in the mood.

Me: "Why are you showing me this?"

Jude: "I was set to go to jail but got probation instead, so I can't afford to get into trouble again. That's why I avoid going out, especially to parties. If the police get involved, my career could be at risk."

The article on an insensible act finally made sense to me. Yet another unexpected situation ambushed me, earning a spot in my vast New York collection of startling moments and epiphanies. Sensing my need for solitude and reflection, Jude departed that morning, breaking our usual tradition of a leisurely sleep-in together.

Now, even two decades later, I write this with a heart still heavy with confusion. Apple sorting was usually easy-peasy for me. Good apple... bad apple... but this one apple, it's a mystery I've yet to decipher.

There was more than met the eye of course, secrets that I can't fully disclose. He was portrayed as a cunning deceiver in the article, an accusation he didn't even bother to refute. Was it really an act of love? Was it all an act of love? Only the actor knows.

37

Big Apple Last Love

In my memoir, you'll notice love is a recurring theme. That's because love was my lifeline during tough times. It's my personal testament to the old saying 'love conquers all'. Tim, Simon, Jai, and my sister Kaylee were my pillars of support. Their unwavering support and endless love never failed to uplift me. They've been there through thick and thin, and I hold them close to my heart. Amidst all this, I yearned for a partner, solid as a rock, to share in life's ups and downs.

You might be wondering, what sort of discomfort and crisis could I be talking about? It's the Big Apple, baby. The rosy, red skin is a veneer. You can expect the city to deal you some tough cards. I've tried to keep the emotional exhibitionism low, threw in a few jokes, and took out hearty chunks of harsher experiences. There were times when I was on the brink of being expelled from the country and times when money was so tight I had to skip meals to make rent. Even though I was living in the fancy SoHo, there were days I could only afford to eat in Chinatown.

My work life wasn't always easy either, and I often felt stressed and powerless amidst the complicated power dynamics. I wouldn't categorize myself as a victim, but it's fair to say I've had more than a few hard knocks in the city.

Writing this book was cathartic, allowing me to unpack and let go of some prickly memories. I've always had a knack for taking difficult memories and tucking them away in a closed box, using the lessons they've taught me to move forward. However, writing this book made me break my own rule of 'never looking back'. At times, it was as tough as swallowing a large pill without water.

While living in Amsterdam, I consulted a psychologist who, after several sessions, identified me as having a 'survivor' personality. This was during a significant turning point in my life, and despite having the support of loved ones, I wanted an unbiased and professional opinion to ensure I was making a sound decision.

I just came across an intriguing article by Al Sieber, acclaimed author of *The Survivor Personality: Why Some People Are Stronger, Smarter, and More Skillful at Handling Life's Difficulties... and How You Can Be Too*. The article is titled *The Genesis of the Survivor Personality*. If you identify as a 'survivor' personality, or even if you're just curious to see if you might be one, I strongly recommend giving it a read. Sieber really knows his stuff, so I'll share his list of 'survivor' traits that struck a chord with me:

- (They) have the curiosity of a long-time child who asks: "How does this work?", "What if I did such and such?", "What would happen if I acted in another way?"
- (They) allow their feelings to guide their curiosity.
- (They) are willing to be foolish, make mistakes, get hurt and laugh at themselves.
- (They) may test the limits, break rules or disobey laws to find out what happens.
- (They) carry on conversations with themselves, daydream and have active imaginations. They play in and with their minds.
- (They) can be a cooperative non-conformist, i.e., not being controlled by social mores, laws or standards, and yet choose to abide by the laws and rules.
- (They) are comfortable in and even amused by ambiguous situations that may frighten or bewilder others.
- They seem to like happy endings, good completions.

- (They) maintain a positive direction and show surprising self-confidence against sustained adverse circumstances.
- (They) fall back to and successfully rely on inner resources in disruptive, chaotic circumstances.
- They try to set things right, to clean up bad situations.

Source:

"The Genesis of the Survivor Personality." Al Sieber.
Al Sieber Resiliency Center resiliencycenter.com/
exceptional-mental-health/. Accessed 23 August 2023

My last love in the Big Apple, Phil, put those last three traits to the test. Our relationship was the longest and most intense I had in NYC. He was younger by a few years, which usually isn't a biggie. But let's just say, when you're in your late twenties dating a guy in his early twenties, the maturity gap is wider than the Grand Canyon.

Phil was a walking bundle of contradictions - a macho athlete with a sensitive soul, a lover of extreme sports who could also paint a beautiful canvas, a photographer who captured the world's beauty and a poet who poured his heart onto paper. His head full of wild, brown curls was as untamed as his spirit, but his good nature and charm won over anyone who met him.

Our banter was like a tennis match, with volleys of wit and humor flying back and forth. We could spend hours in an art gallery, museum, in the park or watching a movie marathon, and he fit in perfectly with my circle of friends. "Finally, someone normal, Kimmie!" Tim would tease. With Phil, life was always an adventure, filled with love, laughter, and a dash of the unexpected.

Sounds like a dreamboat? Well, almost. Picture a 'bridge and tunnel' dude from Long Island – that was him, living the island life when Cupid decided to smack us both right in the derriere. Love at first sight? Sure felt like it. We moved in together quicker than a New York minute because, seriously, who enjoys long commutes? Suddenly, the typical SoHo loft parties had a new dynamic duo running the show.

Phil then tossed me into his adrenaline-charged world of extreme sports and outrageously early mornings. I don't surf, but I was more than happy to play the part of the admiring girlfriend as he tamed the waves in Montauk. Whether he was surfing or snowboarding, time seemed to stand still for him. The guy was up at the crack of dawn and only dragged his surfboard back when the moon was high in the sky. Adrenaline, it seemed, was his life force. As for me, a city chick, extreme sports were as alien as country music in my loft.

In the dating world, Phil was a rarity - a man with a car. More specifically, a dilapidated surfer's wagon that, against all odds, still ran. It even survived a break-in on my SoHo street, emerging somehow even more battered. But boy, the road trips were a hoot. Phil played chauffeur on breezy drives to Long Island, New Jersey, Connecticut, and Boston. I used to exclusively hit the road with Kaylee, but now, I had a new co-pilot.

Ever the efficiency expert, Phil had a knack for turning my empty bottles of Snapple Mango Madness into his personal porta-potties on our road trips. I'd get all fiery, but then I'd realize the hilarity of it all. My once Mango Madness was transformed into Golden Madness. Speaking of which, Mango Madness was my go-to thirst quencher in the US.

We often journeyed to Long Island to visit his folks, who treated me like one of their own. His mom was a real gem - full of warmth, wisdom, and a liberal spirit that could engulf you. She had this knack for making you feel right at home with her comforting words. Phil's dad, on the other hand, was a staunch Republican, while his mom was a Democrat. Despite their political divide, their love for each other was evident as long as they steered clear of any political talk.

You know what they say, when life gives you lemons, you make lemonade. But when life gives you a winter cabin in Vermont, like Phil's parents did, you make snow angels. Oh yes, our chilly chill-outs in the cabin were my ticket to commune with Mother Nature in a way that the concrete jungle of Manhattan just doesn't allow. I'd step out of our cabin each morning, get a face full of fresh snow aroma. And then, there was the satisfying crunch-crunch sound my winter boots made as they stomped on the snow-covered ground. But the big city girl in me was always on high alert, especially when we'd hear the rustle of some wild critter as we were out gathering firewood.

But the highlight reel moment? That was when we spotted a moose, right outside our cabin. This majestic creature just stood there, basking in the golden morning sun, a sight so beautiful it could make a postcard jealous. It was a far cry from the honking taxis and bustling crowds of Manhattan, and for a city slicker like me, it was nothing short of mind-blowing.

Phil wasn't just a surf and snow fan, he was also fanatic about turning me into a snowboarding enthusiast. Our first epic lover's spat was about his overzealous snowboarding lesson. He was like a kid in a candy store, desperate for me to share his joy. I agreed to try, because as Al Sieber said, us 'survivors' "are willing to be foolish, make mistakes, get hurt and laugh at themselves." But instead of giggling at my own ineptitude, I was ready to throttle Phil after my first catastrophic snowboarding attempt. Phil might be a hotshot on the snowboard, but he had zero patience.

One fine morning, sun smooching the snow, we were off to this bunny slope, aka 'slopes for dummies'. It was to get a hang of skiing before trying not to break bones on the big boys' slopes. After 30 minutes of more 'fall and rise' drama than skiing on the kiddie slope, Phil got the yawns. He told me to unstrap and lift the board. The next thing I knew, we were queueing for the ski lifts. I was clueless about what was coming up next.

So there we were, hoisted up into the unforgiving sky like a pair of mismatched socks on a laundry line. Below us, once familiar faces were reduced to mere speckles on the earth's canvas. For a while, my mind drifted off to appreciating the well-groomed trails and stunning snow-dusted mountain views. I'd lost count of the minutes we'd been airborne, but it was long enough for me to start mentally writing my will and wondering if I'd left the oven on.

Phil, my personal joy-killer, hollered, "Strap your board on and jump when I say so!" Excuse me, what now? I barely survived the bunny slope and now he wants me to dive off a cliff? How high are we talking? Sadly, my pondering was cut short.

In the misty soup of my brain, the command to "jump!" rang out. Suddenly, I was free falling down a mountain, my confidence trailing behind me like a lost puppy. I was a human snowball, rolling and tumbling down the mountain, each crunch of snow under me echoing my mounting panic.

Landing at the foot of the slope, I was a crumpled snow angel, eyes wide in shock. After a few deep breaths and a moment of silent prayer to the snow gods, I kicked off the cursed snowboard. In swishes Phil, Mr. Snow Pro, sliding to a stop next to me with all the grace of a figure skater. I flung the snowboard at his smug face and stormed off. For the next week, Phil got a taste of the cold shoulder.

Phil kept company with an interesting bunch. They were fresh out of college, still carrying that frat-boy aura around them like a bad cologne. My favorite was Reese, a Filipino American, who was the only one who didn't blend in with the sea of white, crass, unsophisticated, and unfortunately, homophobic guys. He was a jolly, chonky, sweet-as-pie newbie Analyst at some bank. Always on top of politics and the latest gossip, he was the guy that came with a joke in one hand and a beer in the other.

Phil's friends showed up to our wild loft parties with their frat-pack mentality, awkwardly gawking at our diverse group of friends. So, we eventually had to ban them like a bad one-hit wonder. Not that I minded. Less of their Pabst Blue Ribbon beer cans lying around meant more room for the good stuff. You know, champagne, wine, the spirits that don't come in a 30-pack.

On certain nights, I'd meet Phil and Reese for post-work drinks. Once, they hit a swanky Wall Street bar near Reece's bank. By the time I arrived, they were as drunk as skunks. When Phil and his crew reached the 'slurring nonsense' stage, I felt like escaping. Their drunken banter usually devolved into childish gibberish.

Phil had turned into a dipsomaniac. Unemployed and with an abundance of free time, he'd commence his libations right after lunch. By sundown, he had mastered the not-so-subtle art of speaking in slurred cursive. Meanwhile, I was back to the daily grindstone, wearing the shiny hat of a Marketing Consultant. I was rubbing elbows with an Asian non-profit, funded by the Lower Manhattan Development Corporation and September 11 funding. The mission? Buff up downtown businesses with killer marketing strategies. As for advertising, I decided it needed a timeout.

At one point in the night at the swanky Wall Street bar, Reese, in an un-Beerlike fashion, put his beer down and meandered to the loo. Not long after, he came waddling back, grinning like a Cheshire cat. "Guys, you won't believe what I found in the toilet!" he exclaimed. He plonked a mysterious black velvet bag on the table.

Phil and I were all elbows and noses, trying to peek inside as he loosened the drawstrings. And what did we find? A treasure trove of blue round pills. Before I could even ask what they were, Reese was shaking them out into Phil's eager hand. Down the hatch they went, in one swift gulp. Reese did the same, then they both cackled, clearly enjoying their own Beavis and Butthead moment.

"Whoa! What are you doing? You don't know what those pills are!" I hollered. Reese, ever the smarty-pants, retorted, "Sure, I do." Phil, unable to contain his laughter, blurted out, "They're ecstasy pills!" They giggled like sugar-hyped kids with a secret stash of candy. I wasn't convinced they were just 'party pills' and had visions of them turning into projectile vomiting everywhere. If they were what Phil claimed, they had just swallowed a handful. Can you OD on ecstasy pills? I sat there, arms crossed, feeling like a distressed babysitter.

Sixty minutes later, Phil and Reese began to boogie down, morphing into disco versions of National Geographic specials. Their dance moves began to mimic a slow-mo replay, with Reese flinging his arms about like he'd signed up for an aerial yoga class, and Phil, interpreting ocean waves through interpretive dance. As we became the star attraction of the bar, I buried my blushes in my palms.

Suddenly, Phil decided to up the ante. He whipped out a blue pill, promising it was the key to happiness. Under duress, I swallowed it. Like a rollercoaster ride on steroids, my head began to spin, and the floor decided to play a game of hide and seek with me. I was in free-fall, and it scared the pants off me. Phil decided to finally play the responsible adult and got me home in a cab.

When we shuffled back home, we plopped ourselves onto the couch, ready to vibe with the trippy tunes of Hope Sandoval from her Bavarian Fruit Bread album. The enchanting crooner from Mazzy Star has this hypnotic voice, luring us deeper into the hazy world the pills had created. In my valiant quest to understand some mysterious topic during this trippy state, I found my fingers doing a marathon around my hair, twirling it into oblivion for hours on end.

The aftermath wasn't so pretty, especially with the slow, trippy music elevating our feverish state. We eventually passed out on the couch. The next morning, I almost scared myself when I saw my reflection - my hair had transformed into an afro. It took several days, countless washes, and a ton of hair conditioner to finally get my hair back to normal.

Phil's misguided drunk fun quickly got very out of hand. Every day was like groundhog day, with Phil blabbering incoherently like a lost parrot. His mood swings were faster than a speed skater on a sugar high. I tried to turn our home into a 'no booze' zone, but he just shifted his party to the local bars. And if I tried the tough love approach and locked him out, he'd kick the door down.

Over weekends, he would hit the waves at dawn and come back at ungodly hours, acting like he had single-handedly drained a brewery. His favorite magic trick was pulling a Houdini, vanishing without a trace. This self-destructive behavior was set on repeat for months.

We had this grand idea that road trips were the magical band-aid for our romance that was circling the drain.

So we decided to take a trip to Montauk. Our bickering had a better mileage than the car itself, and by the time we reached the hotel, our moods were sour. He decided to drown his sorrows at the bar, turning himself into a human cocktail. He wobbled back to our room, ready to "kiss and make up". I wasn't in the mood for a heart-to-heart when he was tanked. Miffed, he grabbed a fruit knife and threatened a Romeo and Juliet style exit. It was the straw that broke the camel's back.

I confided in Tim, Jai and Aya and they all broke out into a chorus of 'Hit the Road Jack'. I drafted in his parents, and his family hosted a painful intervention. Phil threw in the bar towel and checked himself into the AA's 12-step recovery program. We all heaved a sigh of relief. You see, the first step of the 12 was an acknowledgement of his drinking problem– "We admitted we were powerless over alcohol — that our lives had become unmanageable."

If you've ever loved someone struggling with alcoholism, you know the profound heartache of seeing them slide down a treacherous path of self-destruction. The stark reality is that one in three people succumb to this disease, their lives not the only ones shattered in the process. The ripple effect of alcoholism engulfs the lives of those around them, creating a shipwreck of emotions for those who care for them. As the drink blunts their pain, it only amplifies the suffering of their friends and family. This is a truth I know all too well, as my father was an alcoholic.

Phil returned home. I extended my support, every ounce of strength I had, every bit of courage I could muster. Yet, there came a point where the line had to be drawn, a boundary set - not out of malice, but out of necessity. There's only so much one can do, especially when dealing with the shadows of abuse or loved ones caught in its vicious cycle. This period was incredibly emotional and heartrending for me. Ultimately, the time arrived for me to leave the Big Apple.

38

How Did It End?

On January 18, 2023, Jacinta Ardern resigned as New Zealand's Prime Minister, citing burnout. At the press conference, she announced that she no longer had "enough left in the tank". Her words echoed in the hollow of my being - a poignant reminder of my own exhaustion.

I am far from being a Prime Minister, yet I understood her sentiment all too well. The feeling of running on empty, of your spirit drained, and your energy depleted. It seems inconceivable to feel so burned out in the prime of my twenties, and yet, I did. I am no quitter, but the relentless pace of life in the Big Apple had left me emotionally and physically bankrupt.

How did my heart become this gas tank empty stage? It was the relentless accumulation of heart-wrenching experiences and soul-crushing disappointments in the Big Apple, that triggered a complete emotional collapse. The dream was to thrive, not merely survive. True, there's no thriving without surviving, but the cost was too steep. The never-ending struggle, the constant hustle - it took more from me than it gave.

My turbulent entanglement with Phil, in its final stages, drained every last drop of my emotional reserves, leaving me gasping for breath. Despite the desperate need to sever this connection, I found myself helplessly entwined. My only path to salvation was to distance myself, not just from him, but from this soul-sapping city. He may not have been the sole reason for my emotional bankruptcy, but he undoubtedly was the tipping point.

My time at the non-profit was marred by an unsettling discovery - a scheme to exploit the generosity of funders. The Founder, while promising to assist struggling businesses in the wake of 9/11, was merely paying lip service. I formed a bond with a colleague, Faye, whose background in investigative journalism shone a light on the shadows within the organization. Her relentless pursuit for truth uncovered the layers of deceit and manipulation by the Founder. Today, Faye remains a cherished friend.

The Founder was harsh on us, the underpaid consultants, who worked tirelessly, believing in our cause. We faced the raw emotions of struggling business owners, some even suicidal. After uncovering unethical practices, Faye and I resigned as we refused to be complicit. Despite being from Hong Kong, Faye, married to an American, had the security to stay in New York.

Was I eager to dive into the whirlpool of sponsorship-seeking for my H-1B visa application, twiddle my thumbs for half a year waiting for that golden stamp of approval, shoot myself out of the country only to boomerang right back and press the reset button? No thank you.

I hit the wall of overwhelm. This wasn't your run-of-the-mill burnout you could soothe with a soul-searching sojourn to Fire Island. No, we're not talking about the kind of trip where you recharge your batteries by catching up on your Z's, sipping on swanky cocktails, cloud-watching for funky shapes, or observing the avian version of mealtime. Then, with every body part capable of crossing, crossed, you hope that you've magically bounced back by the end of your stint.

There was more to it than stress and pressure. It wasn't something that just accumulated overnight, or over weeks, or even months. It was a slow and agonizing build, a slow burn, a slow grind that wore me down bit by bit. There were countless papercuts, small and seemingly insignificant, but each one compounded the last, and slowly, I bled dry.

Disengaged and detached, I lost all my strength, all my will to stay on in the city that had once been my sanctuary.

Phil proposed a marriage of convenience to solve my visa woes. Not that he didn't love me, but we were just kids, really, and the road ahead was still long and winding. I wasn't about to let an immigration paper dictate our lives. So, I gave that visa the proverbial bird.

Fast forward to one Saturday night at our regular watering hole, Café Noir. Tim, attempting to muster all his seriousness, tried to engage us in a 'serious conversation'. He couldn't keep a straight face for more than five minutes.

Tim: "Kimmie. Simon and I had a discussion."

Me: "Uh huh."

Tim: "Simon would like to marry you."

Me: "Marry me?"

Tim: "Yes. Then you can get yourself a green card and hang out in New York indefinitely."

It was the sweetest, most bizarre proposal I'd heard in a while. There was a gentle tug at my heart, which had flatlined in recent weeks.

Me: "And you're OK with that?"

Tim: "Absolutely! The three of us get to live together, happily ever after."

End of serious conversation. We cackled at the absurdly simple plan. Sweet as it was, no convenience marriage for me. Two proposals in weeks? I'm the world's luckiest woman.

With a heart brimming with emotion, I made the choice to return to my homeland, letting the metaphorical 'pickaxe' fall. I no longer wish to feel like an uninvited guest, an unwanted outsider. I refuse to be relegated to the status of a third-class citizen, less than even a second-class immigrant. I will no longer justify my worth, my talents, my capabilities in a ruthless competition that doesn't seem to value who I am as an individual. I'm done with apologizing for being a woman with ambitions, as if ambition and femininity are mutually exclusive. I refuse to accept the constant discrimination I face based on my ethnicity in my arduous climb up the corporate ladder.

I am breaking free from these oppressive shackles, leaving behind the toxic environment that has hindered my growth. I am choosing to embrace a new path, seek fresh opportunities. I am choosing to be true to myself, to honor my values, my identity.

Once my decision was made, a torrent of contrasting emotions washed over me - profound sadness mingled with intense relief. Let me assure you, it wasn't cowardice that prevented me from fighting another round, but bravery to acknowledge it was time to retreat. My time in the magnificent Big Apple was vibrant, extraordinary, and memorable, enough to fill the pages of this memoir.

I wanted to take a bite off the Big Apple, only to have her take a bite off me instead. It took me two decades to realize that I hadn't failed. It's not the success but the courage to stay on and survive the Big Apple that matters.

I had triumphed in ways I never expected. I was left with the gift of lifelong friendships and a deep, meaningful bond with Kaylee, a love that healed our shared scars of a traumatic childhood. I found my place in a new world. I found comfort in crises. I lost and found love. I weathered life's fiercest storms, each one leaving me stronger, more resilient. The setbacks and failures shaped me into the survivor I am today and will forever be.

So I kickstarted the beginning of the end. I broke the news to the Kaylee, Jai, Aya and the gang. They were shocked, yes, but they'd been on this crazy ride with me, so they got it. Next on the agenda was my landlord. I negotiated my way to an early lease termination. There I was, my last 30 days ticking down like the final seconds of an intense game of musical chairs.

I had to chuckle when I thought back on Al Sieber's list of 'survivor' personality traits, especially the one about liking happy endings. Well, in my goodbye month, the crew decided to only hit straight bars, just for my happiness. Every time we hung out, they were all in denial about my departure. They kept thinking I'd pull a fast one and yell, "Gotcha!"

The scene in my loft was as chaotic as a raccoon in a trash can - there was Kaylee, my sister, showing up day after day to help me cram my life into cardboard boxes. Now, Kaylee isn't one to wear her heart on her sleeve, but I knew she adored our SoHo sisterhood. She even managed to squeeze in a final Thelma-and-Louise-style road trip to Massachusetts, just for kicks. Kaylee was sad about my leaving. Always the stoic one, she slapped on her brave face like it was going out of style. It's a skill she'd perfected back when Mom thought love was a contact sport. And now, I was about to be not just a tunnel, but an entire continent away.

The final curtain was about to drop on the Jai and me saga. After Brooklyn beckoned, his lifestyle did a 180 and he graced us with his presence only for the "Gang's Special". One bright day, the gang, Jai, Kaylee, her hubby and I planned a farewell picnic at Central Park. Jai tagged along his soon-to-be missus, who later turned into his used-to-be missus. Kaylee's husband, with his homophobic tendencies, still showed up. Major props to him, as it was probably less "picnic in the park" and more "trip to the dentist" for him.

After our picnic, Jai dropped the bomb - his lady love, now fiancé, wasn't a fan of our buddy-buddy situation. So, she laid down the law - it was her or me, and let's face it, I can't compete with that diamond ring. So, we had to call it quits on our friendship. He's still in my heart though, and now, permanently inked in this memoir.

I hosted a wild farewell bash at my swanky SoHo loft, my memory-making fortress at 349 West Broadway. The thought of shipping everything back to Singapore was a no-go for me. So, I turned the party into a grab-what-you-can bonanza. Everyone could nick whatever they fancied from my pad. Knowing that everyone had a bit of me to remember gave me the warm fuzzies. Tim constantly ribbed me about my over-the-top winter coat collection, even outdoing the Russians and Siberians. I bequeathed to him a few of the most lavish ones, the ones with fur trims.

Phil was the only one turning on the waterworks at the party, with everyone else with their heads stuck so far in the sand of denial, they half expected me to declare, "I've changed my mind, I'm not going."

So, the day arrived when I had to bid adieu. My flight was scheduled to depart at 10 in the morning. Meanwhile, my gang of night owls found themselves begrudgingly crawling out of bed at the unholy hour of 5:30 a.m. A night of revelry that left us nursing a collective hangover. But, for our resident early bird, Kaylee, it was just another day. She drove all the way from Edison, New Jersey to scoop me up at 6 a.m.

The drive to JFK Airport was long, and to kill time, I regaled our early bird with tales of our nocturnal escapades. She seemed to enjoy our stories, although I had my suspicions about whether she was actually listening or just nodding along. The enormity of my impending departure hadn't quite sunk in yet. It felt like I was just stepping out for an extended holiday, not leaving for good.

With an hour to spare before my flight, the gang and I decided to have a final hoorah at a 24/7 watering hole, bright and early at 7 a.m. Even Jai and Phil showed up. The crowd was a bunch of solitary sippers nursing their last beers, with a few snoozing at their tables. The bartender, probably bored out of his mind, seemed thrilled to see some fresh faces.

We took a trip down memory lane, reminiscing about all our ridiculous stories. Despite the collective hangover, spirits were high and got even higher when Simon, the genius, suggested shots. I lost count after five, but I'm pretty sure we went way past that. Kaylee, the queen of stoicism, didn't utter a peep over drinks, even though you could practically see her heartbreak radiating like a neon sign. Meanwhile, Phil was the human embodiment of a waterfall, crying so hard we had to keep him from flooding the bar. Tim, ever the comforter, tried to be the human dam.

For the grand finale, Tim and Simon unveiled a large-sized gift that at first glance seemed like a frame for a really big fish. But no, it was a collage of our misadventures, a testament to our crazy years together. I tried keeping it out, but every glance became a sob-fest, so into the closet it went. After all, we're supposed to be moving forward, not swimming in nostalgia.

Kaylee was the group's timekeeper, probably the only sober one among us. She knew we were a few drinks away from becoming human pretzels. And then, like Cinderella, I had to dash off for my flight before I turned into a pumpkin.

Stumbling up to the security checkpoint, we were as jolly and loud as a bunch of drunken Santas at a Christmas party. What a spectacularly dignified exit, I'd say. I gave everyone a big, sloppy bear hug and a smooch before I wobbled my way through security. I spun around for one last look, waving with the enthusiasm of a kid who'd just discovered how to use their hand.

The final memory of my farewell was as colorful as a circus. There they were, faces as red as beetroot, drunk as skunks, throwing kisses and waving like they were trying to flag down a UFO. Kaylee finally let the floodgates open but still managed to smile and wave like a beauty queen on parade. Phil was bawling his eyes out while Tim, ever the rock, held him up like a human crutch.

Just as my flight was about to depart, I hastily took my seat, my hands trembling as I struggled to fasten my seatbelt. The plane began its rumbling journey down the runway, a tangible reminder of the journey I was about to undertake. My eyelids fluttered shut, the faces of my loved ones at the security gate etched behind them. A flood of warm tears broke free, cascading unchecked down my cheeks as memories enveloped me.

I felt the wheels of the plane lift off, the solid ground slipping away beneath us. The deafening thud as the pilot retracted the wing flaps echoed in my ears like a heartbeat, a harsh reminder of the reality I was leaving behind. As the plane ascended, my heart pounded in sync with the rising altitude. I could almost see it in my mind's eye, the nose of the plane pointing defiantly upwards, challenging the vast sky. It was a comfort, a reassurance that despite the bumpy ride that awaited me, I was still moving forward, still rising.

As the ground disappeared beneath the sea of clouds, I realized I was embarking on a new chapter of my life.

About the Author

Kim Lee, a former Chief Marketing & Digital Officer and Executive Creative Director, is on her career break in Singapore. A recipient of 27 global marketing and advertising awards, she's written her first book, a memoir, and is thrilled to cross it off her bucket list.

Printed in Great Britain
by Amazon

49558522R00176